A BRIGHT
ROOM
CALLED
DAY

A BRIGHT ROOM CALLED DAY

TONY KUSHNER

THEATRE
COMMUNICATIONS
GROUP

ISBN 1-56865-110-4

A *Bright Room Called Day* was first presented by Heat & Light Co., Inc. in a workshop production at Theatre 22 in New York City in April 1985. Tony Kushner directed the following cast:

AGNES EGGLING	Priscilla Stampa
BAZ	Stephen Spinella
PAULINKA ERDNUSS	Alexandra Rambusch
ANNABELLA GOTCHLING	Maria Makis
VEALTNINC HUSZ	Peter Guttmacher
ROSA MALEK	Kimberly Flynn
EMIL TRAUM	Jonathan Rosenberg
DIE ALTE	Theresa Reeves
AH*	Tracy Martin
GOTTFRIED SWETTS	David Warshofsky
ZILLAH	Roberta Levine
ZACHARY*	Michael Mayer

*Characters died in the rewrites.

The play premiered in San Francisco at the Eureka Theatre in October 1987. Oskar Eustis directed the following cast:

AGNES EGGLING	Sigrid Wurschmidt
BAZ	Jeff King
PAULINKA ERDNUSS	Carmalita Fuentes
ANNABELLA GOTCHLING	Abigail Van Alyn
VEALTNINC HUSZ	Michael McShane
ROSA MALEK	Ann Houle
EMIL TRAUM	David Warshofsky
DIE ALTE	Jaime Sempre
GOTTFRIED SWETTS	David Warshofsky
ZILLAH	Lorri Holt

In January 1991, *Bright Room* was produced at the Joseph Papp Public Theater by the New York Shakespeare Festival. Michael Greif directed the following cast:

AGNES EGGLING	Frances Conroy
BAZ	Henry Stram
PAULINKA ERDNUSS	Ellen McLaughlin
ANNABELLA GOTCHLING	Joan MacIntosh
VEALTNINC HUSZ	Olek Krupa
ROSA MALEK	Angie Phillips
EMIL TRAUM	Kenneth L. Marks
DIE ALTE	Marian Seldes
GOTTFRIED SWETTS	Frank Raiter
ZILLAH	Reno
ROLAND	Kenneth L. Marks

The play benefited immeasurably from the editing and dramaturgical advice provided by Kimberly Flynn, Carl Weber, Ellen McLaughlin and Oskar Eustis. Through frequent discussion with Oskar Eustis the shape of the play has changed substantially since its first incarnation; this version incorporates many of his structural ideas and suggestions.

Thanks also to Mark Bronnenberg for his keen eye and loving support.

A Bright Room Called Day is for Carl Weber, teacher, mentor and friend; for Kimberly Flynn, a true and triumphant heroine in the face of great adversity; and is dedicated to the memory of Florence Kushner: Zeicher tzadikah livrachah.

CHARACTERS

AGNES EGGLING: mid- to late 30s; preferably heavyset. Bit player/character actress in the German film industry.

GREGOR BAZWALD (BAZ): early to mid-30s. Homosexual who works for the Berlin Institute for Human Sexuality.

PAULINKA ERDNUSS: mid-30s, but looks a little younger. Actress in the German film industry; a featured player on her way to becoming a minor star.

ANNABELLA GOTCHLING: mid-40s. Communist artist and graphic designer.

VEALTNINC HUSZ: mid-40s. Cinematographer. Hungarian exile. Missing an eye, he wears spectacles with one lens blackened.

ROSA MALEK: mid- to late 20s. Minor functionary of the KPD (Kommunistische Partei Deutschlands).

EMIL TRAUM: mid- to late 20s. Slightly higher-ranking functionary of the KPD.

DIE ALTE: a woman, very old but hard to tell how old—somewhere between 70 and dead-for-20-years. White face and rotten teeth. Dressed in a nightgown, once white but now soiled and food-stained.

GOTTFRIED SWETTS: ageless; when he looks good he could be 30, when he looks bad he could be 50 (or more). Distinguished, handsome, blond, Aryan.

ZILLAH KATZ: contemporary American Jewish woman. 30s. BoHo/East Village New Wave with Anarcho-Punk tendencies.

PRODUCTION NOTES

A Bright Room Called Day is set entirely in Agnes Eggling's apartment, a small flat in a large nineteenth-century residential building in a low-rent district in Berlin. The apartment has probably no more than three rooms. Only the main room is visible. It is cluttered, cozy and has large windows.

Zillah's table, overburdened with books, should be to one side.

A detailed, realistic apartment set will weigh the play down and give the audience the wrong signals (that this is a realistic account of a period in history). There should be something wonderfully warm and inviting about the place, and something verging on the fantastical. We should be able to recognize it as an apartment, but not in any sense an ordinary one.

The play relies on being grounded in emotions to make its points and have its effects. At the same time, it doesn't work at all as a mumbly domestic drama; the language needs attack, precision, specificity, and needs to be moved along with confidence and fearlessness. And politics are true passions for these people, not pretexts for private feelings.

Editing is possible throughout, and recommended. In Scene 23 I have sentimentally restored a speech of Baz's, which in most productions has been cut. The entire speech, which begins "Do you remember ten years ago, Agnes?" and concludes "Goodnight. Paris awaits," can and probably should be deleted (keeping only the very last line).

The impulse to interrupt the Weimar-era play with Zillah Katz's editorializing—and she is not the playwright—came from a curiosity about the necessity of metaphorizing political content in theatre. Why, I wondered, shouldn't audiences hear an unapologetically didactic, presentational voice as well as representational scenes? The result of this question, and the solution that is Zillah, make for the most interesting and problematic aspect of the text.

The present version of the play uses earlier versions of Zillah's interruptions—mostly from the Eureka Theatre production. I have appended to the back of this volume the interruptions we used for the New York Shakespeare Festival production; there's something to be said for either version.

The German scenes have remained essentially unchanged throughout the several drafts of *Bright Room*; Zillah's materials have gone through drastic revisions (originally she had a brother—and in the London production she was an anti-Thatcherite Brit). Ideally there should be a continual updating of the specifics of Zillah's politics of paranoia, in the form of references to whatever evildoing is prevalent at the time of the production. Though I think she should stay true to the zeit informing her particular geist, namely the Reagan-era, there might be politically useful emendations made, if *intelligently* done, and never without my approval.

A third possibility, one not yet attempted in any of the play's productions, is to do the play without Zillah. I have heard the script read this way, and I consider performing the play without interruption an interesting solution, though I believe it makes the play less difficult and possibly less dangerous. It would certainly be less likely to freak out critics. Whether or not that's a good thing, I leave to the individual reader or producer.

The slides are essential; the scene titles aren't meant to be printed or projected, but can be if the director wants.

The photograph of the Nazi rally referred to in the stage directions and by Zillah in Act II is an actual photograph. It is printed in *Hitler: The Pictorial Documentary of His Life* by John Toland (Ballantine Books, New York, 1980).

A parliamentary government was established in Germany in 1918 following the human and military disaster of World War I. The Weimar Republic was a constitutional democracy, Germany's first experiment with the form, in which authority was divided between an elected President, an elected national parliament (the Reichstag), regional parliaments and a Chancellor (roughly equivalent to a Prime Minister) appointed by the President to shape and oversee workable parliamentary coalitions. The Republic survived attempts by the German Army High Command to seize power, as well as a failed communist revolution in 1919 and several aborted fascist coups during the '20s.

For most of its existence, the Weimar government was marked by its inability to arrive at stable parliamentary coalitions. The Reichstag was stalemated time and again, and the President repeatedly dissolved it. While the parties of the Right moved closer to cooperation and political solidarity, the main powers of the German Left, the gigantic Social-Democratic Party (SPD) and the German Communist Party (KPD), were entirely unable to form a United Front to stop the rise of Fascism. Instead, the SPD wasted critical time and energy seeking common ground with the Right, while the KPD's energies were increasingly strangled by interference from the Comintern, Moscow's international directorate.

The National Socialist German Workers' Party (the Nazis) grew from political obscurity to prominence in the early 1930s. In 1932 they became the largest voting bloc in the Reichstag, having received 37.5% of the popular vote in the July parliamentary elections. Although their popularity began to decline immediately after this, and though the KPD's popularity began concurrently to rise, the Nazis were able, through the support of the conservative and Catholic center parties, and of the military and major industrialists, to secure from aging President Hindenburg the appointment of their leader, Adolf Hitler, to the post of Chancellor of the German Reich.

You know, upon our German stages,
Each man puts on just what he may;
So spare me not upon this day . . .
So in this narrow house of boarded space
Creation's fullest circle go to pace
And walk, with leisured speed, your spell
Past Heaven, through the Earth, to Hell.

> —From the Prologue in the Theatre, Goethe's *Faust*,
> translated by Walter Arndt

The Republic had too much in common with its enemy;
the spirit of revenge for Versailles, the fear of communism . . .
But above all the Republic was aware of its own tediousness.
The people wanted theater.

> —Heinrich Mann, quoted in
> *The Brothers Mann* by Nigel Hamilton

"You'd be surprised how much being a good actor pays off."

> —Ronald Reagan
> May 1, 1984

PART ONE

EVENING MEAL IN A WINDSTORM

(Lights up on Zillah at her table, reading. Repeated slides of a huge crowd rallying in support of Hitler, everyone giving the fascist salute. With each slide the people in the crowd draw nearer, till finally we fix on a single figure, a woman who isn't saluting. Zillah looks up, holds up the book she has been reading.)

Slide: JANUARY 1, 1932.

(Lights up on Agnes's apartment in Berlin. Seated around a table: Agnes, Husz, Baz, Paulinka and Gotchling. It's night; the scene is lit by candlelight. Everyone has been drinking.)

GOTCHLING
Capitalism is a system of . . . of . . .

PAULINKA

Digestion! A digestive system!

HUSZ

We've drunk too much.

GOTCHLING

Again.

HUSZ

(To Gotchling) You hold your liquor. I admire that. Did you know . . .

GOTCHLING

What?

HUSZ

Did you know that candlelight aids the digestive processes?

GOTCHLING

Yes. I knew that. And the fennel in grapeskins helps you see in the dark, but wine makes your gums shrivel prematurely.

BAZ

I think I'm going to vomit . . .

PAULINKA

Ah! The advantages of opium.

AGNES

Midnight.
HAPPY NEW YEAR!

(General exultation, "Happy New Year!")

AGNES

Oh . . . *(Laughs)*

GOTCHLING

What?

AGNES

Oh my . . . *(Laughs)*

BAZ

What? What?

AGNES

All of you. Look at your faces. It's a kind of perfect thing, like a circle, a round perfection.

GOTCHLING

Cheap sentiment. Cheap geometry. Time for coffee.

AGNES

No! I feel . . . what? Baz, what do I feel, I feel . . .

BAZ

Do you feel warm, Agnes?

AGNES

Yes.

BAZ

And , , , complete, Agnes?

AGNES

Complete? Mostly.

BAZ

Safe?

AGNES

Well . . .

BAZ

Relatively safe?

AGNES

We live in Berlin.
It's 1932.
I feel relatively safe.

HUSZ

Sufficient for the times.
(He stands up)
Now I would like to propose a toast.

GOTCHLING

Excellent ideas! A man of ideas! Propose, Husz.

HUSZ

To Agnes!

GOTCHLING

To Agnes! Good-hearted and brave!

HUSZ

Occupant prima of our affections, immovable tenant of this small, solid room: health, happiness and relative safety on this fierce and splendid night and for many years to come, dear heart.

EVERYONE

To Agnes.

(Silence.)

PAULINKA

And in the silence, an angel passed over.

BAZ

Now what to do to begin the new year properly?

GOTCHLING

You were going to vomit.

BAZ

Yes, but now I have a better idea. Let's make up a story.

HUSZ

What kind of story?

Baz

One we compose together. A story about . . . something.

Gotchling

About a cold night.

Paulinka

A story about a cold night. Good. I begin.

Baz

Please! This is Agnes' party. Agnes' apartment. Agnes should begin. Begin, Agnes.

Agnes

Oh, let's see. . . . Ha!

There was a winter once in Berlin when a terrible wind, cold as death, chased people through the streets at night and blew ice into their bones and killed them. Well there was one man who had to walk to work late every evening . . .

Gotchling

He was a night watchman. And he said to himself, "This wind is murder." And he decided to spend his last hard-earned penny on a thick woolen coat and an extra-long scarf and then the night wind could blow all it liked, he'd be warm and safe. "Our humanity," he said to himself, "is defined through our struggle to overcome nature." So he did buy those things, and . . .

Paulinka

And he wore them at night on his way to work, and the wind saw what he was up to, and it grew very angry and sharp, and it blew all the harder, and in seconds flat the man felt so cold he might as well have been naked. Score one for nature.

Gotchling

One for nature.

BAZ

And he knew his plan had failed, and the wind was killing him, so with blue and frozen lips he prayed to God to save him from the wind, but of course God didn't, and he caught a severe influenza.

HUSZ

And as he lay on his deathbed, he thought he heard the wind whistle, "Just you wait." His new coat and scarf hung from a peg on the wall. He could feel his life slipping away. He said to himself, "I wonder what's next?" and as he died he could hear the wind calling . . .

(Gotchling blows out the candles.)

AGNES

"Just you wait."

(In the darkness, everyone laughs. End of scene.)

Slide: JANUARY–JUNE 1932.

Slide: POLITICAL TENSION.

Slide: FIERCE FIGHTING, SOMETIMES IN THE STREET.

Slide: CRISIS/TRANSITIONAL PERIOD/CHANGE.

Slide: THE ISSUES ARE PARLIAMENTARY & REVOLUTIONARY.

Slide: THE WEIMAR COALITION IS A SHAKY AFFAIR.

Slide: AN UNEASY MARRIAGE OF LEFT-LIBERALS AND MODERATES.

Slide: IN APRIL, PRESIDENTIAL ELECTION.

Slide: HINDENBURG DEFEATS HITLER.

Slide: JANUARY–JUNE 1932.

LOVE SCENE
WITH LEMON

Slide: MAY 30, 1932.

(Agnes listening to the radio: jazz. Husz enters.)

AGNES

Let's have sex.

HUSZ

Wait. A surprise.

AGNES

What?

(He pulls a lemon from his pocket, hands it to her.)

AGNES

Oh, a lemon! God, I haven't had a lemon in months! You shouldn't have, Husz, they're so expensive . . .

Husz

Courtesy of the Studio. I stole it from the set. I pretended to be fiddling with the fruit bowl arrangement and . . . *(Demonstrates pocketing the lemon)*

Agnes

Let's have sex.

Husz

Not tonight.

Agnes

But I'm anxious tonight and I need to.

Husz

But I'm anxious too and I don't want to.

Agnes

Can I have a kiss?

Husz

Of course.

(They kiss.)

Agnes

I got a film.

Husz

How much?

Agnes

The rent at least. It's going to be a miserable film, swan-boats and parasols. I play a wise old lady-in-waiting for the Kaiserin. Jolly twinkles. Want to see a jolly twinkle? *(She twinkles)*

Husz

Today on the set they were complaining about the lack of good ideas for new films. I suggested we make one about men from

Mars: They live off the pus produced by bodily infections. They're covered with enormous boils, they have runny noses and eyes. The director says no, Germans don't want to see films about disgusting creatures like that, they want to see films about Germans. I said, "Herr Director, you simply do not understand the principle of metaphor."

AGNES

You shouldn't tease them; Germans are sensitive.

Husz

Not sensitive, insane. And never jolly. Present company excepted, I hate all Germans.

AGNES

Marx was a German.

Husz

Marx was a Jew. With a London address. And the soul of a Hungarian. I should never have left Hungary.

AGNES

They threw you out

Husz

I should never have left Russia.

AGNES

If you wanted to stay in Russia you shouldn't have read Trotsky.

Husz

Read Trotsky, hell. I *knew* Trotsky. Goddamned Trotsky. In Russia we were making great films.

AGNES

But if you'd stayed there you'd never have met me: my sensual compensations for artistic mediocrity. Just a quick . . . ?

Husz

I'm too anxious.

AGNES

Thanks for the lemon.

HUSZ

Small pleasures in bad times.

(End of scene.)

ALL DAY IN THE RAIN

Slide: MAY 30, 1932.

(Lights up on Agnes and Paulinka.)

PAULINKA

His name is Dr. Bloom. He's a Jew with a big belly and bushy
eyebrows. He has a red leather couch and a little picture of
Freud framed in gold. I lie back and pretend I'm in Vienna.

AGNES

Sounds romantic.

PAULINKA

It's unspeakably erotic. He has hair, dark hair, on the back of his
hands. On his knuckles, like a wolf!

AGNES

What does he say about the opium?

PAULINKA

He doesn't know about that yet.

AGNES

I thought that was the point, the opium.

PAULINKA

No, not the *point*, this is psychoanalysis, there is no *point*, nothing so vulgar as that. The opium's mine. None of his business, really. Or yours.

AGNES

Then why bother?

PAULINKA

Because I am unhappy. Because I have to do *something* with all this money they pay me. Psychoanalysis makes more sense than communism. At least I don't have to pretend to read thick books with greasy pages and tiny print. At least I don't have to call sweaty people I don't like "comrade." At least I *belong* on a couch. You don't have a political bone in your body.

AGNES

I do so. Apparently. Apparently I do.

PAULINKA

You didn't used to.

AGNES

I've changed.

PAULINKA

You aren't a communist.

AGNES

Not yet, but.
I was walking to the Studio, you know, past that office they have, the storefront on Leopold Street, and I stopped and I looked in the window, you know, the posters, the red flags, and I felt my

lungs go all tight and I thought, well. . . . And I walked in and said, "Hello I'm Agnes Eggling and I want to join the Party."

PAULINKA

Just like that. Bang.

AGNES

Well I've been thinking of doing it for a couple of months but basically bang, yes. Of course you can't just join up but they seemed very interested; I told them I was an actress and they asked me to do a skit.

PAULINKA

You'll make a fool of yourself.

AGNES

For the Transport Workers Strike Rally. Well not for the main rally but for sort of a . . . side rally.

PAULINKA

People throw things at strike rallies. This is a phase. You'll recover. Even I was a communist once.

AGNES

Impossible.

PAULINKA

Oh yes, full party membership. It lasted about two weeks. The communists make the best films, so I thought I'd sign up and then after the revolution I'd get all the good parts.

AGNES

And what if the Nazis made the best films?

PAULINKA

The Nazis? Their films are all about mountain climbing.

AGNES

But if they did.

(Paulinka gives the Hitler salute.)

AGNES

Pig.

PAULINKA

Pig yourself.

AGNES

Paulinka.

PAULINKA

Oh I know. I disappoint you. Well I disappoint myself. I do. But what can I do, I do what I can. Nothing compared to the Martyrdom of Red Agnes, Thespian for the Revolution, but . . .

AGNES

Last night I went to a big meeting. A man was giving a speech. I don't know who he was but he said things. That here is where capitalism will take its final stand. Here, in Germany. Not in twenty years, or forty, but soon. Today. If we go red the whole world will follow us. Everything bad and dangerous swept away.

PAULINKA

Imagine that.

AGNES

How can I stand back from that, Paulinka?

PAULINKA

I can't imagine.

AGNES

Paulinka, these are the most exciting days of my life.

(End of scene.)

FIRST INTERRUPTION

THE SMALL VOICE
(LETTER TO THE PRESIDENT)

(Lights up on Zillah.)

ZILLAH

Dear Mr. President,

I know you will never read this letter. I'm fully aware of the fact that letters to you don't even make it to the White House, that they're brought to an office building in Maryland where civil-servant types are paid to answer the sane ones. Crazy, hostile letters—like mine—the ones written in crayon on butcher paper, the ones made of letters cut out of magazines—these get sent to the FBI, analyzed, Xeroxed and burned. But I send them anyway, once a day, and do you know why? Because the loathing I pour into these pages is so ripe, so full-to-bursting, that it is my firm belief that anyone touching them will absorb into their hands some of the toxic energy contained therein. This toxin will be passed upwards—it is the nature of bureaucracies to pass things vertically—till eventually, through a network of hand-shakes, the Under-Secretary of Outrageous Falsehoods will shake hands with the Secretary for Pernicious Behavior under the Cloak of Night, who will, on a weekly basis in Cabinet meet-ings, shake hands with you before you nod off to sleep. In this way, through osmosis, little droplets of contagion are being rubbed into your leathery flesh every day—in this great country of ours there must be thousands of people who are sending you poisoned post. We wait for the day when all the grams and drams and dollops of detestation will destroy you. We attack from below. Our day will come. You can try to stop me. You can raise the price of stamps again. I'll continue to write. I'm saving up for a word processor. For me and my cause, money is no object.

Love,
Zillah.

(She puts letter in envelope, licks and seals it, smiles)

(End of interruption.)

LATE NIGHT STRUGGLES ON TOWARDS DAWN

Slide: MAY 30, 1932. LATE NIGHT.

(Agnes is alone, working on the skit. She has pencil, paper, various materials including the Red Baby—a doll—and a little Hitler doll.)

AGNES

(Writes, then reads out loud) Red Workers! Red Berlin! Arise! The world is perched on the brink of doom! *(She scratches out "doom," then writes, then reads)* The world is perched on the brink of a catastrophe! *(She scratches out "catastrophe," then writes, then reads)* The world is perched on the brink of a choice. The brink of a choice? Stupid. Stupid. Perched on the brink of . . . shit. *(She goes to the radio, turns it on: jazz music. She goes back to the table, picks up the little Hitler doll)* Hello. I'm Adolf Hitler. Thank you for inviting me here on this lovely May morning. I love jazz. I love the dance music of dark-skinned peoples. Jewish wedding

music. I love that! Dance with me! *(The doll dances a bit)* Vote for me! Kiss my ass! Watch me fly in my aeroplane! Look up! Here I am! *(She makes propeller noises and flies the little doll about the room. Then she crashes it with great relish)* RED WORKERS! RED BERLIN! ARISE! THE WORLD IS PERCHED ON THE BRINK OF . . . SOMETHING. . . . CHOOSE! COMMUNISM OR FASCISM! THE REVOLUTION OR DEATH! STRIKE! NOW! REVOLUTION! NOW!

HUSZ

(Running in from the bedroom) Who are you screaming at?

AGNES

I'm working on the skit.

HUSZ

Work more quietly. I'm trying to sleep.

AGNES

Husz, what are we perched on the brink of?

HUSZ

Come to bed.

AGNES

Perched on the brink of . . .

HUSZ

Fascism. Old age. Senility. Sleep.
(He goes back to the bedroom, slams the door)

AGNES

(Returning to the table) Thanks.
(She picks up the lemon, cuts it open, sucks on it)
Mmmm. Sour fruit.

(End of scene.)

DIE ALTE
(THE OLD ONE)

Slide: MAY 30, 1932. AN HOUR AFTER MIDNIGHT.

(The apartment is very dark. Agnes is asleep at the table. Die Alte opens the window from without and comes into the apartment. She sits opposite Agnes.)

DIE ALTE

I remember the day: a sky
so bright that beneath it
every thought is drowned, save
innocence. Summer
but the sun's a chill apricot light,
high up,
a dense, brilliant haze—an immense
day . . .
War was declared.

Which war, I don't remember.
We wore corsets then;
rigid with the tusks of whales;
they pinched, and often
bruises and blood. But
that was a wonderful time.
I heard the snap of the flags
crack in the wind, and the men marched past.
Something hot moved through me that day,
up through the ribs of the corset—
it was my heart. I remember that.
A wonderful time, not
now . . .
Now. Hungry. Always. Never
enough.

(Agnes stirs in her sleep.)

DIE ALTE

(With quiet fear) Ahhh . . .

COLD AND BRUTAL BUT EXACT AND TRUE

Slide: JUNE 2, 1932.

(Agnes is alone with a glass of wine, struggling with the opening pages of Das Kapital. *Baz enters without knocking, followed by Gotchling.)*

BAZ

Guess where we've been.

AGNES

Where?

GOTCHLING

At a Nazi rally.

AGNES

You didn't.

BAZ

In Wedding. "Red" Wedding, I think you people call it. Now it looks more like Nazi Wedding. *(He produces a swastika pennant which he waves about)*

AGNES

You went inside?

BAZ

We stayed for practically the entire event! You must have an intimate knowledge of the enemy.

GOTCHLING

He's apparently done this before. He thought I should see it happening firsthand.

AGNES

See what happening?

BAZ

The floodgates breaking open. The sewers backing up. *(To Gotchling)* Tell her what you saw.

GOTCHLING

A year ago I designed a series of posters for the Party office in Wedding.

BAZ

Which the Nazis blew up last month.

AGNES

It's being rebuilt.

BAZ

They'll blow it up again.

GOTCHLING

Tonight I recognized at least ten "comrades" whose faces used to decorate KPD functions. Devout communists. Now they're wearing swastikas.

BAZ

Right. Like bugs to a gas lamp. The Nazis make more noise, so bzzzzz. They attract the most insects. Fine specimens of Germanity, looking high and low—well, low, mostly, for any release for their desperately trapped sexual energies.

GOTCHLING

Oh not this crap again . . .

BAZ

Well they won't find it in the Communist Party. Membership requires a doctorate in hypocrisy. Let's see, which leg are we going to stand on this week, the left or the right? Can't decide? Call Stalin!

GOTCHLING

Ah, political clarity from the Institute of Human Depravity.

BAZ

Sexuality! Human Sexuality.

GOTCHLING

You know dear just because they employ you doesn't mean you have to *listen* to their ridiculous theories. If sexual frustration was the cause, everyone would be a fascist.

BAZ

Glib reductionist.

GOTCHLING

Sex maniac. *(To Agnes)* He was a socialist until he discovered his penis; then he became an anarchist. *(Back to Baz)* Half of those people at that rally tonight think the Nazis are socialists. Half of the Nazis *are* socialists! This is no party, no ideology, just a shabby collection of borrowings from all over—a bad collage. When Hitler reveals himself as just another flunky for German capital, the working class will abandon him.

AGNES

They'll destroy him.

GOTCHLING

Absolutely!

BAZ

Economic analysis! So antiseptic! So sterile! The fascists don't
try to make sense. They abandon morality, money, justice—
Hitler simply offers a lot of very confused and terrified and con-
stipated people precisely what they want, a means of release.
These people are far beyond caring whether Hitler is a socialist
or not. They're in love with the shine on his boots, they want a
fatherly boot heel to lick, they want him to say "Daddy loves his
children, now go and kill for me." They're completely deaf to
your hairsplitting pseudoscience and jolly-comrade goodwill.
They want bloody things.

GOTCHLING

Baz, you're a slob, an intellectual slob.

BAZ

Ouch. And I thought I was being marvellously eloquent, pene-
trating to the very heart of the Mystery of the Decade.

GOTCHLING

Wallowing in coffee-klatch bullshit. Without economics it all
turns to drivel. You're never going to make a coherent political
theory based on orgasms. The capitalist system is disintegrating:
inflation, devaluation, murderous unemployment, collapse.
These people are frightened because the capitalists can't tell
them how to save themselves and they haven't heard us yet.
They will. The preconditions for revolution are in the making.

BAZ

Why do I detect a note of uncertainty?

GOTCHLING

You don't. I know it will look bad till then. People will make a lot of mistakes. A drowning man clutches at twigs.

BAZ

Yes. But this particular twig may very well save them.

AGNES

(Scoffing) Hitler? How!?

BAZ

Once he's Chancellor he'll build an army and start looking for a war. Guns make jobs, right, comrade? It won't be hard convincing Hindenburg or the German people. Germans love guns, more than jobs. And before . . .

AGNES

Not true! The system can't recover from the Crash!

BAZ

Says who?

AGNES

Everyone. It hasn't yet. Its decline is Historically Inevitable. And for another thing, the German proletariat doesn't want war.

BAZ

I submit, Agnes, that you are a middle-class actress who knows very little about the German proletariat.

AGNES

I know enough. And I submit, Baz, that you are a condescending snob whose homosexuality alienates him from the proletariat.

BAZ

Indeed?
(To Gotchling) Is she learning this from you?

AGNES

And your theories, by the way, of sexual repression as the root
of all evil are half-baked.

BAZ

Half-baked. This from a Marxist who's never read Marx!

AGNES

I have so!

BAZ

The *Communist Manifesto* doesn't count. Everyone's read that!
And my being homosexual brings me into contact with more
proletarians than you can imagine.

AGNES

So does working at the Studio.

BAZ

Right. They paint your face and clean up after you've finished
acting. I have sex with them.

GOTCHLING

And they tell you they're voting for Hitler?

BAZ

Some do.

GOTCHLING

Do you still sleep with them?

BAZ

I'll never tell.

AGNES

Baz!

BAZ

What?

AGNES

You'd sleep with a Nazi?

BAZ

I didn't say that. You sleep with a Trotskyite.

AGNES

That's different.

BAZ

Not to Stalin it isn't.

AGNES

Evasion.

BAZ

I have to get to work.

AGNES

More evasion.

BAZ

No but I do. The Institute is doing a big poster campaign. Abortion on demand. Free condoms. Great big posters. The Nazis will adore them. In the face of an erupting volcano we struggle hopelessly, hopelessly . . .

AGNES

Not hopelessly.

BAZ

Who can say? Prophecy is sorcery, sorcery is a sin.

GOTCHLING

More slop, Baz. You are the victim of a mental illness that deflects admirable energy into bad romantic posturing. It'll be money in the end, you wait—capital for the fascists and the workers for themselves. Bad time to be wasting time. Join the Party.

BAZ

I can't.

GOTCHLING

Why not?

BAZ

They won't let me wear mascara. Good night. *(He exits)*

AGNES

(To Gotchling) Do you think he sleeps with Nazis?

(End of scene.)

Slide: JULY 21—NOVEMBER 6, 1932.

Slide: IN JULY, PARLIAMENTARY ELECTIONS.

Slide: THE NAZIS WIN 37% OF THE POPULAR VOTE.

Slide: THIS IS THE LARGEST GENUINE VOTE THEY WILL EVER RECEIVE.

Slide: THEY NOW WIELD A PARLIAMENTARY MAJORITY.

Slide: THE COALITION OF LIBERAL-CENTER PARTIES,

Slide: THE "WEIMAR COALITION,"

Slide: HAS BEEN DEFEATED.

Slide: THEN, IN NOVEMBER, MORE PARLIAMENTARY ELECTIONS.

Slide: COMMUNISTS GAIN 12 SEATS, THE NAZIS LOSE 34.

Slide: A SHARP REVERSAL IN FASCIST POPULARITY IS WIDELY PREDICTED.

Slide: BUT THE NAZIS STILL CONTROL A PARLIAMENTARY MAJORITY.

FINGERSPITZENGEFÜHL (FINGERTIP FEELING)

Slide: JULY 21, 1932. NATIONAL REICHSTAG ELECTIONS.

(Agnes and Paulinka sit over toast and coffee at the table.)

PAULINKA

She met him at a fancy-dress dinner a year ago. Nazis and tycoons. She was this close, and she swears to me that his little black moustache is not made of hair.

AGNES

What's it made of?

PAULINKA

She couldn't tell. Something hard and shiny. Beetle wings, who knows.

AGNES

That's ridiculous.

PAULINKA

You hear all sorts of things. You know that in Munich he developed an incestuous infatuation for his cousin. He forced her to live with him and a whole lot more besides. She killed herself. She was seventeen. And at the Studio I heard from someone who has a brother high up in the Party that every woman who winds up in his bed either kills herself or has an accident or is found murdered later.

AGNES

Oh that's nonsense.

PAULINKA

You don't believe it? I do.

AGNES

Who wants to know about his perversions?

PAULINKA

They say he's a coprophiliac.

AGNES

A what?

PAULINKA

Shit.

AGNES

OH PAULINKA, PLEASE, THAT'S DISGUSTING!

PAULINKA

I didn't make it up. This woman told me that she actually knows a high-priced prostitute who spent the night with him. She won't talk about what happened or what's got her so scared, but now she's in terror for her life. She rarely leaves her flat these days and she always feels cold.

AGNES

I don't want to hear anymore.

PAULINKA

Agnes, do you believe in evil?

AGNES

It's not something you believe in. There are evil men, of course.

PAULINKA

Diabolical evil?

AGNES

What are you asking me?

PAULINKA

Do you believe in the Devil, Agnes? That's what I'm asking you.
Do you believe in the Devil?

AGNES

At my age?

PAULINKA

Because I do.

(End of scene.)

IT TAKES THREE
INVITATIONS

(There is a sudden change of lighting: the room grows dim, and a brilliant spotlight hits Paulinka, who warms to it immediately and begins to address the audience.)

PAULINKA

I've seen Him. Well, not Him, exactly, or . . .
When I had just started acting I did two seasons at the Municipal Theatre of Karlsruhe. Ever been to Karlsruhe? *(She smiles; it is a telling smile)* We were giving *Faust, Part One*, a play I've always detested, and I was playing Gretchen, a part I've always detested, and I was not happy, not happy at all. There were nights I thought I'd be stuck in the provinces forever, never see Berlin, never see the inside of a film studio, die, go to hell, and it'd be exactly like Karlsruhe. Black nights, you could imagine your whole life gone . . .

You know the scene in the play where the black poodle turns into the Devil and offers Faust the world? All that demurring, endless, always seemed so coy to me. Just. . . . But so one night I was walking home after a performance and a very strange thing happened. I found myself going down a narrow street, an alley, really, one I'd never been down before, and suddenly. . . . There was this little black poodle, sitting on a doorstep. Waiting for me. Staring at me with those wet dark dog eyes. And I thought to myself: "It's Him! He's come to talk to me!" He's going to stand up on His little hind legs and say "Paulinka! Fame, films, and unsurpassable genius as an actor in exchange for your immortal soul!"

And that's when I knew it, and my dears I wish I didn't know: I'd never resist. I couldn't. I am constitutionally incapable of resisting anything. A good actress, a good liar, but not in truth a very good person. Just give me Berlin, sixty years of success, and then haul me off to the Lake of Fire! Do business with the Devil.

But the poodle had other things in mind. I guess I must have startled it when I asked it if it wanted to make me an offer. It *leapt* up at me, barking and snarling and obviously out for blood. Chased me for blocks. I escaped by ducking into a bar, where I drank and drank and drank . . .

Probably just somebody's nasty black poodle. But I've always wondered . . . what if it really was Him, and He decided I wasn't worth it?

(End of scene.)

DEMONOLOGY

Slide: SEPTEMBER 12, 1932.

(Agnes alone, sitting with Das Kapital, *flipping the pages distractedly. There is a loud knock. She goes to answer it.)*

MALEK

(Entering) Comrade Eggling, we come as specially designated representatives of the Party's Central Committee. We've been sent to convey congratulations to you and your comrade collaborators for a highly successful agitprop performance.

AGNES

Oh well thank you that's very . . .

TRAUM

(Entering behind Malek) Long live the Revolution! Long live Germany!

AGNES

YES! Yes. Can I get you some . . . tea or . . .

MALEK

We hope you'll continue to contribute your efforts to the struggle.

AGNES

Oh absolutely. I mean, I intend to. I don't usually, but . . . well, as much as I can. Absolutely, I . . .

TRAUM

Good.

One other matter and then we can be going. There are certain Left-deviationist tendencies in your play that must be corrected before it can be performed again. Which hopefully will be very soon.

AGNES

Left-deviationist tendencies?

MALEK

Small problems, really.

TRAUM

Well, not so small . . .

MALEK

Fairly small.

TRAUM

Actually fairly large.

MALEK

Fairly small.

(Tiny uneasy pause. To Agnes) It would be more appropriate, in keeping with current Party policy . . .

TRAUM

(Consulting a notebook) Look. This is the play about the Red Baby?

AGNES

Right. The Red Baby Play.

TRAUM

Highly amusing. The Red Baby. . . .What is the Red Baby, comrade?

AGNES

It's . . . well, it's a symbol . . . a symbol of . . . of . . .

MALEK

A symbol of nascent communism in Germany.

AGNES

Right!

MALEK

Of the newborn proletarian revolution.

AGNES

Exactly.

TRAUM

Exactly.

AGNES

What?

TRAUM

Exactly. Exactly the problem. Look, comrade, as you probably already know the most recent directives of the Comintern Executive have . . .

(Agnes isn't understanding a word.)

TRAUM

How to say this.

MALEK

Comrade Eggling, the focus of your play is very clearly the proletarian revolution in Germany, that it's going to happen very
soon.

AGNES

Yes.

MALEK

Well the difficulty is . . .

TRAUM

(Simultaneously) Exactly. And that is no longer an accurate reflec-
tion of the policy of the Comintern, nor of the KPD.

AGNES

It isn't?

TRAUM

No. It is Left-deviationist adventurist opportunism.

(Agnes doesn't get it.)

TRAUM

You're rushing things.

AGNES

You mean there isn't going to be a proletarian revolution?

TRAUM

Oh, well, eventually, yes, but . . .

MALEK

(Simultaneously) Well of course there has been one in Russia. In
Germany . . . eventually, yes. But it's not necessarily the next
step.

AGNES

What's the next step?

TRAUM

Defense of Soviet Russia.

AGNES

But in Germany? Here?

MALEK

Well, a United Front against Fascism . . .

TRAUM

But *not* with the Social Democrats.

MALEK

No. No. Not with the Social Democrats.
(Again a tiny, uneasy pause)
Well what we mean by that is . . .

TRAUM

(Simultaneously) Well, with the Social Democrat workers but not the leaders. The SPD leadership must be exposed as Social Fascist and hence indistinguishable from the Nazis.

MALEK

Well, *not* indistinguishable.

TRAUM

Oh yes.

MALEK

No.

TRAUM

Yes! The Comintern's position on this . . .

MALEK

You're wrong! Not even the Comintern is stupid enough to say that.

TRAUM

Oh yes they are!

MALEK

You're wrong, comrade.

TRAUM

(Pulling rank) NO! YOU are!

(There is a very uneasy pause.)

TRAUM

We feel certain that in time the workers loyal to the SPD will come over to us.

AGNES

It looks like more of them are going over to the Nazis.

MALEK

True.

TRAUM

No! Not true! I mean it looks that way but . . .

AGNES

If there's not going to be a United Front with the Social Democrats then who are you going to be united with?

TRAUM

Look. It's not our fault. They don't want us either.

AGNES

Maybe you should stop calling them fascists.

TRAUM

But they are fascists.

AGNES

No they're not.

TRAUM

Yes they are.

MALEK

No they're not!

TRAUM

MALEK!

MALEK

Well you know the same as I do. They aren't.

TRAUM

As comrade Malek knows perfectly well, holding a firm line against bourgeois parliamentary dictatorships is essential to the revolution.

AGNES

But there isn't going to be a revolution!

MALEK

Oh yes there is!

AGNES

He said there wasn't.

MALEK

Well, he's wrong.

TRAUM

NO YOU ARE!

MALEK

NO YOU ARE!

(Silence.)

AGNES

Just tell me what to do with the Red Baby.

MALEK

We're not artists, comrade. You work it out. Try to deemphasize the importance—the immediate importance—of revolution. The workers aren't ready yet.

AGNES

(To Malek) Do *you* believe this, comrade . . .

MALEK

Malek. Rosa Malek. No. But I believe in Party discipline.

TRAUM

I noticed.

We would also suggest that the Red Baby not be identified as proletarian. We're trying to sell the new concept of the KPD as a party for everyone, not just the workers. "Class struggle" seems to scare the petty-bourgeois right into the arms of the Nazis.

AGNES

I'll do what I can.

MALEK

Thank you, comrade. We appreciate it.

TRAUM

It's extremely important.

AGNES

It's just a skit.

TRAUM

No. Every effort from every corner brings us closer to victory.

(Tiny uncomfortable pause. Traum leaves.)

MALEK

You know, comrade, your play gave me nightmares.

AGNES

It did?

MALEK

The Red Baby. I don't mean this as a criticism but it's awful when you think about it, a *red* baby. Imagine a real red baby. Wouldn't that be horrible, like someone had painted it or boiled it or something.

AGNES

What was the dream?

MALEK

I can't remember. There were several. It smiled a lot, maybe it grew. But it was a nightmare because I woke up all tangled in the sheets.

(Malek gives Agnes the KPD salute. Agnes returns it. They stare at each other. Malek exits. End of scene.)

SCENES FROM THE LIFE: FIRST PART

Slide: NOVEMBER 6, 1932. SECOND NATIONAL REICHSTAG ELECTIONS.

(Agnes is listening to the radio for election news. Gotchling enters with her portfolio.)

AGNES

Twelve new seats! We got twelve!

GOTCHLING

I know.

AGNES

And they lost thirty-four! Thirty-four fascists out the door! Millions of votes! They're losing!

GOTCHLING

(Taking materials out of portfolio) Help with . . .

AGNES

WE WON! We're going to win! Up and up! And I feel like I helped, like I actually moved in time, the lump moved!

GOTCHLING

Cut this along the blackened edges. And be careful.

AGNES

Gotchling! You MUST be happy tonight! Even you!

(Small pause.)

GOTCHLING

My father had a little speech, we'd get it every night after he'd read the papers. "People are pigs" he'd say. "Human history isn't the story of the good man, not of the saint, but of the swine who bludgeoned the saint to death. Fond of mud, full of shit, pigs. In my many years on earth, this is what I've learned." Every night while he ate his onions, word for word. He couldn't let go of it—that contempt or despair or whatever the hell it was. "People are pigs." And last week when I thought the Nazis were going to *add* thirty-four seats I found myself saying "people are pigs," like a chant.
But then they surprise you. The People. Five million come out of their rooms and they vote communist. Which is not easy for them to do. Five million people.

(Husz enters without knocking.)

GOTCHLING

(Suddenly, at the top of her lungs) FIVE MILLION PEOPLE, HUSZ!

(Husz pulls two enormous bottles of vodka from inside his coat.)

Husz

Tonight, we swallow our differences.
Fire, Annabella. In the street, in our throats, in the sky. Red fire.
The ground is shaking.

Gotchling

FIRE!

Husz

I have felt this before. The masses are on the move.

(End of scene.)

SCENES FROM THE LIFE: SECOND PART

Slide: NOVEMBER 6, 1932. LATER THE SAME NIGHT.

(Husz, Agnes and Gotchling, who is working on a collage, cutting and pasting. No one is drunk, but everyone's been drinking.)

Husz

Scenes from the life of Vealtninc Husz, one-eyed cameraman: Russian Episodes. One: I make Trotsky weep.
Interior shot, overhead pan of huge crowd milling, the Red Artists Congress in Leningrad, 1921.
(He hums the opening notes of "The Internationale," then) Dolly in to big knot of people surrounding comrade Trotsky, mingling; track along behind him till he reaches the great Dziga-Vertov. Close up on handshake: the marriage of politics and art. Trotsky notices among DV's entourage a young Hungarian with an eye patch; asks Dziga-Vertov, "This Hungarian, what happened to

his eye?" DV replies, "His name is Husz, he lost it in the revolution in Budapest, comrade Trotsky." Close up on Husz, his black eye patch; jump to closeup of eye of Trotsky, behind its thick, magnifying lens. Looking at Husz. Trotsky: with a big wet tear in his eye.

(Pause; he gets another drink) Music!

GOTCHLING

(Singing)
Arise, ye prisoners of starvation,
Arise, ye wretched of the earth.
For justice thunders condemnation,
A better world's in birth.

HUSZ

Two:
Huge closeup, the mouth of Dziga-Vertov, thin-lipped, saying "Film is the perfect medium, the only medium for the age of machines, because it is mechanically made, uses mechanical construction, montage, juxtaposition, not focused on the small inner life but on the grand scale, capable of recording an entire revolution!" Jump to the ear of Husz, deep, empty, listening, filling up. Interior shot, from the ear to the heart.
(Little pause)
In German film studios, nobody listens.
Music!

GOTCHLING

(Singing)
No more, tradition's chains shall bind us,
Arise ye poor, no more in thrall.
The earth shall rise on new foundations,
We have been naught, we shall be all!

Husz

Three: Dream sequence, like from Hollywood.

(Gotchling starts whistling a high-pitched, dreamy "Internationale" chorus.)

Husz

Map of Europe, borders drawn in black, heavy lines.
Flames eat it up, revealing, behind it,
carved in granite, the lovely word
"Internationalism."
Cross-fade to a magnificent expanse,
a bowl-shaped valley,
mountains,
and millions of people, simply millions,
so many that the valley is completely filled,
each an infinitely precious part of a glorious entirety—
in complex, dissonant, harmonious voice,
Comrades, together, calling Paradise
home.

(Husz sings, then Gotchling, and then Agnes join in.)

ALL THREE

(Singing)
'Tis the final conflict;
Let each stand in their place;
The Internationale
Unites the human race.
'Tis the final conflict;
Let each stand in their place;
The Internationale
Will be the human race!

Husz

End of film.

(End of scene.)

Slide: NOVEMBER 6—JANUARY 1, 1932.
Slide: STAGNATION AND SINKING.
Slide: THE LEFT'S EARLY VICTORIES ARE NOT EXPANDED UPON.
Slide: THE CATHOLIC CENTER SHIFTS ALLIANCES
Slide: TOWARDS THE FASCIST RIGHT.
Slide: BIG MONEY SUPPORT FOR A HITLER CHANCELLORSHIP.
Slide: A DIM AND OPPRESSIVE AWARENESS AMONG THE PEOPLE
Slide: THAT THE BATTLE HAS TURNED
Slide: AWAY FROM THE STREETS AND THE BALLOT BOX
Slide: TO SECRET DEALS BETWEEN POWERFUL PEOPLE
Slide: IN PRIVATE ROOMS.

SCENE EIGHT

ICH HABE EINE NEUE GIFTSUPPE GEKOCHT (I MADE A NEW POISON SOUP)

Slide: NOVEMBER 6, 1932. EVEN LATER.

(The room is dark; Die Alte is at the table again, grinding. Agnes enters from the bedroom, turns on the light. Die Alte looks up at Agnes, who is startled.)

AGNES

Oh!

DIE ALTE

Do you have something to eat?

(Agnes hesitates, staring, then moves to the cupboard and takes an apple from a bowl. She puts it on the table.)

DIE ALTE

Something softer? Cheese?

AGNES
Do you live here? In this building?

(Small pause. Die Alte looks at Agnes.)

DIE ALTE
There's an iron stairs outside the window.

AGNES
The fire escape?

DIE ALTE
Do you have something to eat? The price of things. It's unbearable.

AGNES
You came down the fire escape?

DIE ALTE
The wind's strong there. I press up against the bricks, they're cold, my gown whips against the railing, my cheeks burn. Bread if you don't have cheese.

(There is a loud metallic knock in the walls.)

AGNES
The water pipes.

DIE ALTE
Sounds like knocking. Little penny man. Let him in.

AGNES
(Back to the cupboard) I think I have some rolls.

DIE ALTE
Just before I fall asleep,
After God has heard my prayers,
Things below begin to creep:
The penny man is on the stairs.

AGNES

Oh, I remember that poem, years ago . . .

DIE ALTE

The rolls, please.

(Agnes gives her a roll. She begins to eat, greedily.)

DIE ALTE

It's a little stale.

(End of scene.)

SECOND INTERRUPTION

THE POLITICS OF PARANOIA

(Lights up on Zillah.)

ZILLAH

I used to be a normal human being. Like most Americans of my class I would fatten and thrive on governmental scandals, as long as they were relatively infrequent and bloody enough when they occurred to alleviate the ennui of being a citizen in a two-party democracy. Watergate was one of the happiest times of my life, really well-done, dramatic and garish and incredibly funny. Not at all like the bone-naked terror of these days. I've lost my sense of humor. I have become instead a completely convinced, humorless paranoiac. I see elements of profound truth in nearly all the Kennedy assassination theories. If you tell me that Happy Rockefeller, John Paul I and John Lennon were killed by a cabal of lapsed-Catholic anti-Trilateralists, I will believe you. People who don't know that this government survives by the grace of a secret club of trained WASP terrorists are living with their heads in pink clouds. I believe, I do believe it. Hannah Arendt says she escaped from Germany before the war by being more paranoid than her friends. She read detective novels. She believed in conspiracies. They said she was crazy then but Hannah died in 1972 in her own bed and lots of the people who laughed at her. . . . I believe. I read the histories of Germany. I read the Book of Revelations. I read the *Times*. I sense parallels. Just call me paranoid.

(End of interruption.)

LOVE SCENE
WITHOUT LEMON

Slide: DECEMBER 4, 1932.

(Agnes alone, Das Kapital facedown on table. Radio playing jazz. The music stops and Hitler's voice comes on. Agnes switches the radio off. Husz enters in a hurry.)

HUSZ

Now let's have sex.

AGNES

Not now, I don't want to.

HUSZ

But I need to. I'm anxious tonight.

AGNES

I can't. I'm too anxious.

HUSZ

We have to get together on this.

> AGNES

Kiss.

(They do.)

> AGNES

Did you enjoy that?

> HUSZ

Not particularly, no.

> AGNES

They say he'll be Chancellor. Hindenburg is very old.

> HUSZ

(Tired, with little conviction) There'll be uprisings. His government will be short-lived.

> AGNES

For a thousand years.

> HUSZ

(Laughs) Nothing ever lasts that long.

> AGNES

Lately I feel like I'm in a film, all the time. A newsreel. I see all these events already on film, not just Hitler, but us: no sex, eating and crying. All public events. There is a title: "PERCHED ON THE BRINK OF A GREAT HISTORIC CRIME."

> HUSZ

Indeed.

> AGNES

And you want to have sex? At a time like this?

> HUSZ

I'm anxious.

(End of scene.)

THE RENT

Slide: JANUARY 1, 1933.

(Agnes alone. It's late at night. The apartment is dimly lit.)

AGNES

I can see myself living here
through a hurricane or fire—
even if the building was burning
I think I'd stay.
Why?
Do you know how hard it is
to find an apartment in Berlin?

(As Agnes continues to speak, beautiful, intense sunlight begins to stream through the windows.)

AGNES

I feel at home.
My friends like it here,
better than their own apartments.
I'm not a fool.
I know that what's coming
will be bad,
but not unlivable,
and not eternally,
and when it's over, I will have clung to the least last thing,
which is to say, my lease.
And you have to admit, it's a terrific apartment.
I could never find anything like it if I moved out now.
You would not believe
how low the rent is.

(End of scene.)

Slide: JANUARY 30, 1933.
Slide: PRESIDENT HINDENBURG
Slide: APPOINTS ADOLF HITLER
Slide: CHANCELLOR OF THE GERMAN REICH.

ORANGES

(Agnes and Baz. Night. Baz is kneeling on the floor, praying.)

BAZ

I see no reason to be ashamed. In the face of genuine hopelessness one has no choice but to gracefully surrender reason to the angelic hosts of the irrational. They alone bring solace and comfort, for which we say, in times of distress, "Hosannah and who needs science?"

AGNES

But then you're saying it's all right to admit defeat.

BAZ

Well, when one is defeated . . .

AGNES

But see, that's just the problem. How do we know? What if we lie down and give up just at the moment when . . .

BAZ

When what?

AGNES

When the whole terrible thing could somehow have been reversed.

BAZ

Do you really think it can? The farmers say, "If we could grow wheat in the winter then we wouldn't be so hungry." But does that mean anything to the groundlock and the frost? No. So the farmers wait till spring. What we need is a Meteorology of Human History. Then maybe we could weather the changes in the political climate with as much composure as we weather changes in the weather. Seasons of History. Does it matter if we know why it rains? It just rains. We get wet. Or not. Life is miserable. Or not. The sun shines, or it doesn't shine. You can explain these things, scientifically, meteorologically, and we can applaud the elegance of your explanation, but it won't stop the weather, or that telling feeling of being overwhelmed. Because on this planet, one is overwhelmed.

AGNES

Gotchling would call that defeatist crap.

BAZ

Gotchling. Gotchling is out at this very moment nailing posters to telephone poles. But you and I . . .

AGNES

I remember once I was out all day in the rain, and the sky was dark from morning on, but just before night the rain stopped, and between the black sky and the ground there was a small open space, a thin band of day that stretched across the rim of the world. And as I watched, night came and the ground and sky closed shut. I'm overwhelmed. I feel no connection, no kinship with most of the people I see. I watch them in the underground come and go and I think, "Are you a murderer? Are you?" And there are so many people.

BAZ

Yesterday I was on my way to buy oranges. I eat them constantly in the winter, even though they cost so much, because they prevent colds. On my way to the grocer's I passed a crowd in front of an office building; I asked what was going on and they showed me that a man had jumped from the highest floor and was dead. They had covered the man with tarpaper but his feet were sticking out at angles that told you something was very wrong. There was a pink pool of red blood mixed with white snow. I left.

At the grocer's I felt guilty and embarrassed buying these fat oranges for myself only minutes after this man had died. I knew why he had jumped. I thought of him opening the window, high up, and the cold air . . .

On my way home I reimagined the whole thing, because I felt a little sick at heart. The dead man was sitting up in the snow, and now the tarpaper covered his feet. As I passed by I gave him one of my oranges. He took it. He stared at the orange, as though holding it could give him back some of the warmth he'd lost. All day, when I closed my eyes, I could see him that way. Sitting in the snow, holding the orange, and comforted. Still bloody, still dead, but . . . comforted.

AGNES

I'm not very scientific. I really believed once that oranges prevented colds because they store up hot sunlight in the tropical places they grow and the heat gets released when you eat one.

BAZ

I consider that a perfectly scientific explanation, and probably correct. These are cold days, not to be believed.

(End of scene.)

FURCHT UND ELEND
(FEAR AND MISERY)

Slide: JANUARY 30, 1933. LATER THAT NIGHT.

(Agnes, Husz, Paulinka, Gotchling and Baz. The wreckage of an unhappy evening lies scattered about.)

GOTCHLING
It's all so much dry rot and fungus! The times are what we make them.

HUSZ
And we will make them unlivable.

BAZ
Touché.

GOTCHLING
Things may get tough for a bit.

HUSZ

A bit?

GOTCHLING

More than a bit.

HUSZ

A very long time. To be replaced by something that looks like progress but will turn out to be worse than what it replaced. *(He starts for the bedroom)*

GOTCHLING

Where are you going?

HUSZ

To piss. Out the window. *(Exits)*

PAULINKA

I once said to Rollo Jaspers, "If you didn't fill your films with such hateful, stupid people the world wouldn't look so bad to you." And he said, "I fill my films with the kind of hateful, stupid people the world is full of. Look around you." And at that precise moment, everyone in the vicinity was remarkably hateful and stupid and I had to concede the point. Depressing memory.

GOTCHLING

Opium is the perfect drug for people who want to remain articulate while being completely trivial.

BAZ

I'm off. It's been a lovely wake. Happy eternity, give my best to the corpse.

GOTCHLING

You shouldn't go out.

BAZ

I know, but the tea gardens, my dear. The night is calling.

GOTCHLING

They're celebrating.

BAZ

I want to celebrate too. The end of a very long and painful struggle. Never knew it'd be such a relief!

GOTCHLING

Sometimes . . .

BAZ

Yes?

(Husz reenters from the bedroom.)

GOTCHLING

(To Baz, very angry) I could strike you.

(Silence. Baz goes to Gotchling, kisses her forehead, and exits.)

GOTCHLING

All of you. This elegant despair. You pretend to be progressive
but actually progress distresses you. It's untidy, upsetting.
Fortunately it happens anyway.

HUSZ

So I believed. I journeyed to the home of progress. I gave it an
eye. Progress ate it up, crunch crunch, and said, "You have two
eyes, give me another!" And I said, "Oh no thanks, I'm leaving."

GOTCHLING

And so you left and turned into a reactionary.

HUSZ

No. I didn't. I can't become a reactionary because that eye, part
of me, is to this day lying in the belly of Progress and it will never
let me go. The eye I have left looks clearly at all the shit in front

of it, but the eye I gave to the revolution will always see what it saw then . . .

GOTCHLING

That was the good eye. This one's diseased. Too much Trotsky!

HUSZ

The last true revolutionary, may God keep him! Everyone else has surrendered.

GOTCHLING

Morbid dry rot! I hate arguing with you, Husz. I used to enjoy it, but you've become a bitter old bore.

HUSZ

Sweet Annabella.

PAULINKA

We are such rotten people.

AGNES

No. Don't say that.

GOTCHLING

We may be. History will move on without us.

PAULINKA

We are frightened and faithless. What's inside is an unstable, decomposing mess. Everyone on the street, looking tidy, just thin-skinned vessels full of gray, reeking, swampy pulp . . . *(She starts to get nauseated)*

HUSZ

Listen!

(Everyone except Paulinka is immediately alert. Gotchling goes to the window.)

HUSZ

Do you hear something?

GOTCHLING

No, I . . .

HUSZ

Listen, Paulinka . . .

PAULINKA

What? I don't . . .

HUSZ

Shut up. Listen.
There is something calling, Paulinka.
If you still retain a shred of decency
you can hear it—it's a dim terrible
voice that's calling—a bass howl, like
a cow in a slaughterhouse, but
far, far off . . .
It is calling us to action, calling us
to stand against the calamity,
to spare nothing, not our blood,
nor our happiness, nor our lives
in the struggle to stop the dreadful day
that's burning now
in oil flames on the horizon.

What makes the voice pathetic
is that it doesn't know
what kind of people it's reaching.
Us.
No one hears it, except us.
This Age wanted heroes.
It got us instead:
carefully constructed, but
immobile.
Subtle, but

unfit
to take up
the burden of the times.
It happens.
A whole generation of washouts.
History says stand up,
and we totter and collapse,
weeping, moved, but not
sufficient.

The best of us, lacking.
The most decent,
not decent enough.
The kindest,
too cruel,
the most loving
too full of hate,
the wisest,
too stupid,
the fittest
unfit
to take up
the burden of the times.

The Enemy
has a voice like seven thunders.
What chance did that dim voice ever have?
Marvel that anyone heard it
instead of wondering why nobody did anything,
marvel that *we* heard it,
we who have no right to hear it—
NO RIGHT!
And it would be a mercy not to.

But mercy . . . is a thing . . . no one remembers its face
   anymore.

The best would be
that time would stop
right now,
in this middling moment of awfulness,
before the very worst arrives.
We'd all be spared more than telling.
That would be best.

(Pause.)

GOTCHLING

The most profound thing about you, Husz, is your irresponsi-
bility.
(She heads for the door)
Open the windows, clear the air. I have work to do. A broad-
sheet we're putting out. The United Front. And I'm late. *(She
exits)*

(End of scene.)

THIRD INTERRUPTION

GERMAN LESSONS

(Lights up on Zillah, who holds up a German-language textbook.)

ZILLAH

German lessons. Listen:

"Das Massengrab." Mass grave.

"Die Zeit war sehr schlimm." Times were bad.

"Millionen von Menschen waren tot." Millions of people were dead.

People try to be so fussy and particular when they look at politics, but what I think an understanding of the second half of the twentieth century calls for is not caution and circumspection but moral exuberance. Overstatement is your friend: use it. Take Evil: The problem is that we have this event—Germany, Hitler, the Holocaust—which we have made into THE standard of absolute Evil—well and good, as standards of Evil go, it's not bad—but then everyone gets frantic as soon as you try to use the standard, *nothing* compares, *nothing* resembles—and the standard becomes unusable and *nothing* qualifies as Evil with a capital E. I mean how much of a Nazi do you have to be to qualify for membership? Is a twenty-five-percent Nazi a Nazi or not? Ask yourselves this: it's 1942; the Goerings are having an intimate soiree; if he got an invitation, would Pat Buchanan feel out of place? Out of place? Are you *kidding*? Pig *heaven*, dust off the old tuxedo, kisses to Eva and Adolf. I mean just because a certain ex-actor-turned-President who shall go nameless sat *idly* by and watched tens of thousands die of a plague and he couldn't even bother to say he felt *bad* about it, much less try to *help*, does this mean he merits comparison to a certain fascist-dictator anti-Semitic mass-murdering psychopath who shall also remain nameless? OF COURSE NOT! I mean I ask you—how come the only people who ever say "Evil" anymore are southern cracker televangelists with radioactive blue eyeshadow? None of these bastards *look* like Hitler, they never will, not exactly, but I say as long as they look like they're playing in Mr. Hitler's Neighborhood we got no reason to relax.

I never relax. I can work up a sweat reading the Sunday *Times*. I read, I gasp, I hit the streets at three a.m. with my can of spray paint:

REAGAN EQUALS HITLER! RESIST! DON'T FORGET, WEIMAR HAD A CONSTITUTION TOO!

Moral exuberance. Hallucination, revelation, gut-flutters in the night—the internal intestinal night bats, their panicky leathery wings—that's my common sense. I pay attention to that.

Don't put too much stock in a good night's sleep. During times of reactionary backlash, the only people sleeping soundly are the guys who're giving the rest of us bad dreams. So eat something indigestible before you go to bed, and listen to your nightmares.

(End of interruption.)

WELCOME

Slide: JANUARY 30, 1933. THE HOURS BEFORE MORNING.

(Agnes, Husz and Paulinka. It's the last hour of real darkness before dawn. Agnes has been cleaning up. Paulinka has been sobering up. Husz has been drinking.)

AGNES

A year ago we were better people. It's evil, what's happening. Maybe you were right, Paulinka.

PAULINKA

I doubt it. Right about what?

AGNES

The Devil.

HUSZ

Sssssshhhhh!

AGNES

What?

HUSZ

I don't like loose talk about . . . that. Especially late at night.

AGNES

You're joking. No one really believes in the D—

HUSZ

Want to meet Him?

AGNES

Sure. Why not? You know Him?

HUSZ

Not well, but He'll come if I call.

PAULINKA

You have impressive connections, Husz.

HUSZ

My family comes from the High Carpathians, a village way up on a wild, barren mountain. Goatherds: mean, tough people. In the fourteenth century nearly everyone in the village was butchered, put to the axe for engaging in intimate congress with the Devil. Since then every Magyar born on the mountain has a special understanding with Him. He's very fond of us. He'll come. Should I . . .

AGNES

I already said yes.

HUSZ

Paulinka?

PAULINKA

Of course. I thought I'd have to wait till I died.

HUSZ

First you both have to cover your left eye with your hand.

AGNES

This is silly, Husz. I don't like this.

HUSZ

Quiet please. It's too late. I've already called Him. Cover up,
Agnes.
(He stands suddenly)
Good. (Pause) Music ready?

(There is an answering blast of music: the finale from Mahler's Second
Symphony, The Resurrection. Agnes reacts violently, Paulinka seems
delighted.)

HUSZ

Lights ready?

(The lights become dim and, well, infernal.)

HUSZ

Devil . . . ?

(From offstage and everywhere, a deep voice answers in a whisper—
"Ready.")

HUSZ

Then lights! Camera! Action!

(Blackout. Then two red eyes appear, glowing. It is the Devil's dog. A
strange light begins to fill the room. All the furniture has been
rearranged. A great oak chair, upholstered in crimson velvet, its arm-
rests writhing serpents, has appeared in the center of the room.
Crouching beside it, the Devil's dog, which looks like a mammoth
Dresden china figurine with fiery red eyes; smoke dribbles from its
mouth.

The door swings open and the Devil enters. He is dressed elegantly and walks with a limp and a cane—He has a clubfoot—and He breathes heavily, almost asthmatically.)

HERR SWETTS

Why have you called me?

HUSZ

Thank you for coming. I hope your journey wasn't long.

HERR SWETTS

Not long, no. I have taken up temporary residence in this country. Why have you summoned me?

HUSZ

Friends of mine sensed your presence, wanted to meet you, face to face. This is Agnes Eggling . . .

HERR SWETTS

(To Agnes) Madame. Charmed.

AGNES

(Terrified, speechless) Uhhhh, ahhh . . .

HUSZ

And this is Paulinka Erdnuss.

HERR SWETTS

(To Paulinka) Ah yes. I've seen your films.

PAULINKA

Monsieur, je suis enchantée.

HERR SWETTS

Et moi aussi.
(To Agnes) And you, you are also in films?

AGNES

Uhhh, ahhh . . .

HERR SWETTS

Can she speak?

HUSZ

Usually.

HERR SWETTS

Good. Curing mutes is a messy business. What happened to your eye?

HUSZ

Knocked out by a rifle butt. Hungary, 1919.

HERR SWETTS

That I can fix. May I?

HUSZ

Free of charge?

HERR SWETTS

Oh no, no, never that, never that. A small fee, naturally . . .

HUSZ

Thanks, but perhaps not.

HERR SWETTS

As you wish.
(He becomes slightly more asthmatic, seems a little worried)
Well! So! You have lovely friends, Husz. May I go? *(He starts for the door)*

HUSZ

Oh please, not so abruptly. Leave us a souvenir.

HERR SWETTS

(Becoming rather angry) What? Stink of pitch that clings for years? Hair snarls? I don't dispense souvenirs.

HUSZ

Tell us something.

HERR SWETTS

I don't know anything. *(Again He starts for the door, now audibly wheezing and in evident discomfort)*

HUSZ

A great mystery. The awful secret of these awful times . . .

HERR SWETTS

But really! I know nothing! My ignorance is beyond calculation. It springs from an abysmal font deeper by leagues than the deepest wisdom. I do not know the Workings of the Universe. I only know myself.

HUSZ

That, then.

HERR SWETTS

Auto-biography? *(The wheezing lessens slightly)* It's interminable.

HUSZ

Condense it.

PAULINKA

Yes, please.

HERR SWETTS

(Slight pause, then to Agnes) Might I trouble the mistress of the hearth for a glass of wine? *(On the last words He is hit by some kind of intestinal pain. He heads for the chair)*

AGNES

I . . . I . . .

HUSZ

I'll get it.

HERR SWETTS

Many thanks. And perhaps . . . a little something . . . for my dog. *(Again the pain)*

(Husz pours a glass of wine, brings it to the Devil, who swallows it in one desperate gulp, then drops the glass as He doubles over in terrible pain. He begins to shake and utters a low, dreadful noise, halfway between a moan and a growl. The growl breaks into a shriek as He clutches His heart and begins to speak. His words and His physical pain are a single thing.)

HERR SWETTS

In brief:
I recall a past, nomads, seeming
to them a desert tyrant, with a petty
tyrant's heart,
cruel, greedy, englistered with fat,
fond of the flesh
of children . . .
(Again the intestinal pain; He now seems to be having some awful bowel affliction, alternating between diarrhea and constipation. It gets worse as He speaks)
Years pass;
an Agrarian Phase, I am
rougher, reptilian,
a heart of mildew, dung-heap dweller,
fly-merchant, cattle-killer,
friend . . . of lunatics, Straw
Demon . . . Excremental
Principle, the Shit King!
(There is some kind of release / relief)
Quaint.
Children's stuff.
Years pass, more years,
refinement, Scholasticism,
increasingly metaphysical inclinations

shape me as
a negativity, a void,
the pain of loss, of
irreconcilable separation from Joy, from
God! *(The heart pain returns, worse than before)*
My heart
a black nullity, dull cavity
from which no light escapes,
not an "Is" so much
as an "Isn't." *(The heart pain appears to have stopped)*
Too ethereal. Lacking bite.
(He stands. He appears to be getting stronger)
Years pass, years pile up,
the last century
my heart was a piston pump,
my veins copper tubing,
hot black oil coursed through them,
steam turbines roared.
Very strong! Very hungry!
Flesh of children and much, much more . . .
Heady Days! The best in aeons!
*(He is now standing erect, breathing deeply but without difficulty for
the first time. He mops His brow, straightens His clothing, pats His
hair)*
Even that grows old.
Even yet, years hurtle by.
And in this century, still new,
when questions of form
are so hotly contested,
my new form seems to be
no form at all.
I am simply

unbelievable. Nonobjective.
Nonexistent. Displaced.
Stateless. A refugee.
The accumulation of so much,
the detritus of so many weary years,
I have at last attained
invisibility.
It's not the danger that you see
that's the danger.
I become increasingly diffuse,
like powdered gas taking to air,
not less potent, but more,
spreading myself
around.
(Pause. He breathes)

PAULINKA

Excuse me. This is fascinating. Did you ever consider the possibility that you might be the product of neurotic conflicts? Dr. Bloom says that . . .

HERR SWETTS

No. My rejection of investigation is complete. I preserve my wickedness in its pristine condition. It is never touched.
(As if confiding a secret of which He is immensely proud) I gave birth to Myself.

(Paulinka laughs, charmed. The Devil laughs with her.)

PAULINKA

This isn't meant as an insult, but isn't that a little grandiose?

HERR SWETTS

Grandiose? Ha! Ha! Ha! That's good! Ha! Ha! Ha! Ha ha ha hahahahaha . . .

(His laugh turns into a loud, grotesque, subhuman braying noise which makes everyone move as far from Him as they can. When He stops, He has lost some of His polish and is as we first saw Him—foul-tempered, slightly asthmatic, uncomfortable. He points His cane at Paulinka.)

HERR SWETTS

(Angrily) My dear woman, you cannot possibly begin to imagine how Grand . . . the scope of what's ahead. *(Lowers cane)*
I sense great possibilities in the Modern World. The depths . . . have not been plumbed. Yet.
I haven't talked so much in years.

PAULINKA

And you really are the Devil?

HERR SWETTS

I. . . . My card.
(He hands Paulinka a business card)

PAULINKA

(Reading it) Herr Gottfried Swetts. Hamburg. Importer of Spanish Novelties.

HERR SWETTS

(Beginning to leave) For the time being. Now please excuse me. I really must go.

HUSZ

Of course. Thank you for coming.

HERR SWETTS

(Leaving) Not at all. Take care, Husz. Mind the other eye.

AGNES

Wait!

HERR SWETTS

What?

AGNES

I . . . I . . .

HERR SWETTS

What?

HUSZ

Agnes, don't keep him waiting.

AGNES

I . . . wanted to say . . . thank you . . . for coming and . . . welcome to Germany . . . and . . .

HERR SWETTS

Thank you, madame. And thank you for having me. Most gracious. Goodbye.

(He exits as the last chords of Mahler's Second Symphony explode and the lights go to black.)

END OF PART ONE

PART
TWO

MEMORIES OF YOU

(Cocktail-loungey lights up on Zillah.)

ZILLAH

Music, please.

(Piano intro to "Memories of You." As Zillah sings, slides of Hitler flash behind her. These should be of the "Beloved Führer" publicity-shot variety.)

ZILLAH

Why can't I forget like I should?
Heaven knows I would if I could.
But I cannot get you off my mind.
Though you've gone and love was in vain,
All around me you still remain.
Wonder why fate should be so unkind . . .

Waking skies at sunrise
Every sunset too,
Seem to be bringing me
Memories of you.
Here and there, everywhere,
Dreams that we once knew,
And they all just recall
Memories of you.
How I wish I could forget
those happy yesteryears
That have left a rosary
Of tears.
Your face beams in my dreams
'Spite of all I do;
Everything seems to bring
Memories of you.

(The music tinkles as slides fade out.)

Thanks, Mr. Piano Man.

(End of interruption.)

DER MENSCH IST NICHT GUT—SONDERN EIN VIEH! (MAN ISN'T GOOD—HE'S DISGUSTING!)

Slide: FEBRUARY 27, 1933. NIGHT.

(There is an orange glow in the room, coming through a window from outside. All other lights are off. Die Alte is sitting in a chair at the table, grinding away. Two very loud knocks come from the wall. Agnes enters, turns on a light and stares at Die Alte.)

DIE ALTE

Two knocks.

AGNES

The hot-water pipe. It pours gray water. They have to fix it.

DIE ALTE

Little goblins, penny men. Knock, knock.

AGNES

Oh, that poem. Funny to hear it after all these years; I can still recite it.

DIE ALTE

Memory is like the wind. Tricky. Horrible things forgotten overnight. Pleasant nothings remembered for years.

AGNES

When the tree is black and bare,
And the barren branches droop,
Don't go to the kitchen where
The penny man makes poison soup.

DIE ALTE

When the little penny man
Bangs the pots and pans about,
No one dares to go downstairs,
No one dares to throw him out.

AGNES

(Sniffing) There's that smell again. Have you noticed it in your— where you live? Something rotten, like egg or sulphur gas— maybe something died in the walls.
(She sniffs and tries to locate the smell)
Tonight it's stronger. Smells . . . burnt.
(She goes to the window)
Oh. There's a fire. A building's burning, down in the center. The whole sky's orange. Must be a terrible fire. It's one of the government buildings, with a dome . . . you can't see . . .
(She opens the window to get a better view)

DIE ALTE

When God is good the hours go,
And the sun will melt the snow.
Nothing ever comes that can
Help the little penny man.

AGNES

(Closing the window) It's the Reichstag.

DIE ALTE

Do you have any rolls tonight?

AGNES

The Reichstag is burning.

(End of scene.)

Slide: FEBRUARY 27, 1933. A MYSTERIOUS FIRE.
Slide: THE REICHSTAG BURNS.

FIFTH INTERRUPTION

NIGHT BATS

ZILLAH

Spooky.

Recently when I have succumbed to sleep, my dreams are invaded by a woman dressed in a frumpy hat and coat—and for a change it's not Mom. This woman—I think she came from a book I read—a photograph of a huge crowd, thousands of people, a rally, everyone, and I mean *everyone* giving the fascist salute. But there she is, right in the middle of all these ecstatic people waving their hands, and she isn't cheering, not even smiling, and both hands are clutching her purse and she isn't saluting. I noticed her right off and I guess out of gratitude she came to pay me visits. She's in trouble: she looks old, but she isn't, she's gotten fat and her feet are giving out and her eyes are bad. She hasn't spoken to me yet, but I know she will and when she does . . .

She still can't sleep. Restless, like me. I'm calling to her: across a long dead time: to touch a dark place, to scare myself a little, to make contact with what moves in the night, fifty years after, with what's driven, every night, by the panic and the pain . . .

(End of interruption.)

FURTHER DEMONOLOGICAL EXPLORATIONS

Slide: FEBRUARY 27, 1933. LATER THAT NIGHT.
Slide: THE REICHSTAG IS BURNING.

(Agnes with Malek and Traum. Malek has a carton. Traum is looking out the window.)

TRAUM

It's still going. They should have it out by now.

MALEK

These are things we found at the Party office. We think they're yours. We wanted them out before we get closed down.

AGNES

They won't dare to . . .

MALEK

Absolutely. Any day.

TRAUM

Arrangements have been made. We're ready.

AGNES

For what?

TRAUM

Exile.

AGNES

And then what?

TRAUM

We continue to agitate for the revolution. From without. We wait for fascism to run its course.

AGNES

Which could take how long, do you think?

(No one answers her.)

MALEK

(Taking the Red Baby out of the carton) Look.

AGNES

Want it?

MALEK

Burn it. Burn everything. But don't be seen doing it.
Why did you stop coming around? It's months since. . . . You disappeared. It's not a reproach, I just wondered.

AGNES

Oh, well . . . me? I . . . well I don't know.
(Pause)
When the winter set in, and it got cold. I think there's something wrong, I don't sleep. And this arm, all ice, for . . . hours. It's terrible. Never mind.

When I turn up you know lots of people must be hearing you because I'm always the last to hear. When I disappear, I just . . . couldn't anymore. I'm sorry.

(Little pause.)

TRAUM

The history of our party over the past few years has not been a happy one.

MALEK

For which thank the Comintern. For which thank Moscow.

TRAUM

Malek, please . . .

MALEK

For which thank ourselves for being stupid . . .

TRAUM

Malek, stop.

MALEK

For letting the Russians run our revolution!

TRAUM

Enough!

MALEK

Coward!

TRAUM

Not here!

MALEK

Not ever! Doing little errands while the Comintern . . .

TRAUM

You are appalling! Now is not the time to be attacking the only place on earth where a communist revolution has succeeded.

Blame it on the German working class. Sheep and cattle! Blame it on our own inability to organize! Blame it on the Social Democrats . . .

MALEK

The Social Democrats the Social Democrats!
They didn't kill the United Front. *We did!* Everything determined by what would serve Moscow best. "Hitler may be a fascist but so what, he's less likely to attack Russia than a bourgeois government allied with France!" They *think*.

TRAUM

So I suppose instead we should've campaigned for Hindenburg! Or we should have followed every thug who wanted to turn the Party into the Left answer to the brownshirts. Fight the Nazis on the streets.

MALEK

YES! YES! NOW! SMITE FASCISM WHEREVER YOU MEET IT! Can't you see we're already there? Don't you see how completely overdue . . .

AGNES

Quiet! Please! I have neighbors. The old lady upstairs is a . . .

MALEK

Sorry.
Sorry. Enough.

TRAUM

Excuse us, comrade. We'd better go.

MALEK

Burn everything. Books, pamphlets, everything. But at night. Sift through the ashes. Be careful. *(Exits)*

TRAUM

Were you a Party member?

AGNES

No. Not. I was going to, but . . . no.

TRAUM

Consider yourself lucky. They have the members lists. *(He starts to leave)*

AGNES

I'm . . . I'm sorry.

TRAUM

Don't apologize. It's not your fault, is it? Just do what the comrade says. Burn it all.

(End of scene.)

Slide: MARCH 5–MARCH 15, 1933.
Slide: THINGS GO FROM BAD TO WORSE
Slide: IN NO TIME AT ALL.
Slide: THE GERMAN COMMUNIST PARTY IS OUTLAWED.
Slide: DAILY ARRESTS.
Slide: THE EMIGRATION BEGINS.

KEEP YOU KEEP YOU
I AM GONE OH KEEP
YOU IN MY MEMORY

Slide: MARCH 5, 1933.

(Agnes is cleaning. Paulinka is heard rushing up the stairs. She bursts through the door.)

PAULINKA

Agnes! Agnes!

AGNES

What! Paulinka, what?!

PAULINKA

(Weeping, falling to the floor) The worst, worst imaginable . . .

AGNES

Who? Who?

PAULINKA

Who what?

AGNES

What?

PAULINKA

WHO WHAT?

AGNES

WHO'S DEAD?

PAULINKA

Dead? Who said anyone died. No one died.

AGNES

From the way you're acting I assumed that . . .

PAULINKA

No. No one dead. It's worse than that. The death of love, the death of trust, is worse than death.

AGNES

What are you talking about?

(Paulinka screams, a long, loud wail. Agnes rushes over and claps her hand over Paulinka's mouth.)

AGNES

Have you gone crazy screaming like that? Do you want to have me evicted?

PAULINKA

I got there at 11:30. Tuesday morning, 11:30. I rang his bell. Nothing, nothing. Ring ring, nothing, nothing. The landlady comes out. Waddle waddle. "Oh Miss Erdnuss, it's just too awful, the Herr Professor Doctor. He's gone."

AGNES

Dr. Bloom?

PAULINKA

Poof.

AGNES

Oh Paulinka. How terrible for you. I'm sorry.

PAULINKA

SORRY! Who gives two shits if you're sorry! My analyst leaves
me without a word, without the courtesy of a final session or a
note or anything, right in the middle of everything he just kicks
out the tent poles and leaves with his wretched wife and brats
and leaves me, *me*! That miserable fraud, I'll ruin him. RUIN
HIM!

AGNES

Shut up! Think what you're saying. Why do you think he left?
Why?

PAULINKA

He had no right!

AGNES

Why? Because he's a Jew, that's why, because Germany's not
safe for Jews, because . . .

PAULINKA

THIS IS NO WAY TO TERMINATE TWO YEARS OF
ANALYSIS!

AGNES

Oh you are being selfish and disgusting. Think about him!

PAULINKA

Think about me!

AGNES

No! I don't want to anymore!

PAULINKA

Well thanks so much and to hell with you too! I'll bet he cleared
out his bank account! Bet he took his money!
(She hears herself. Little pause)
Couldn't he at least have told me?

AGNES

Of course not. Obviously not. He had to leave secretly. It's not
easy to get out.

PAULINKA

I don't know what I'll do.

AGNES

Smoke a pipe. Kill tonight. It'll look better tomorrow.

PAULINKA

No, I don't think it will.
This came today. It's a letter from the Ministry of Culture.

(Paulinka offers the letter to Agnes, who does not take it.)

PAULINKA

The film industry is going to be . . . what was the word? *(Consults
letter)* Oh yes; incorporated. I am invited to meet with the offi-
cer in charge, to discuss my plans. They like my work. They
think I have a part to play.
(Pause)
Should I go? What should I do?

AGNES

I don't know. Don't ask me that.

PAULINKA

Will you work for them? Make films for them?

AGNES

I don't know. No. Maybe. No one will care if I do or not. With
you it's different. What would Dr. Bloom say?

PAULINKA

Nothing, probably, he never said much.

No, let's see. He'd say, "Run, Miss Erdnuss, run away from them, you can't live breathing the air they breathe. Meet me in Paris or New York, the strange city they've driven me to. Come find me there. And leave Berlin." That's what he'd say.

(Agnes and Paulinka look at each other.)

AGNES

I don't know. I don't know what to do.

(End of scene.)

SCENE SEVENTEEN

HIC DOMUS DEI EST ET PORTAE COELIS *(THIS IS THE HOUSE OF GOD, AND THESE ARE THE GATES OF HEAVEN)*

Slide: MARCH 12, 1933.
Slide: THE FLAG OF THE WEIMAR REPUBLIC
Slide: IS ABOLISHED.

(Agnes is sitting for a portrait that Gotchling is constructing. Agnes holds a red hammer and a carpenter's level. Gotchling works with a pencil, paper and a variety of assemblage materials. As she works, they talk.)

AGNES

I don't feel like doing this today.

GOTCHLING

I know. I appreciate it all the more.

AGNES

There's no point to this. No point to making posters, they just rip them down. Don't they arrest people for this?
(No answer)

I walked to the Studio yesterday. All the way I felt like I was walking through a strange city, not Berlin. That strange sun not the Berlin sun, too bright. I found myself saying an old prayer for protection . . .

I keep thinking that maybe it wouldn't have been so bad to have been a wise old lady-in-waiting for the Kaiserin. In the films I had lots of well-made objects to handle: a big sturdy clothes brush with stiff bristles, Belgian lace, and there were those silver cases with little enameled hunting scenes on the lids. They were cold but they warmed in your hand and they were heavy. Just holding them made you feel safe. What's so great about democracy?

Want to see a jolly twinkle? *(She twinkles)*

GOTCHLING

Please, that's nauseating.

AGNES

I know you think I'm a reactionary for feeling this way, you judge everyone all the time but I feel it anyway, I feel . . .

GOTCHLING

Feel feel feel feel feel. So much feeling. Hold still. Don't feel. Think for a change.

AGNES

There's nothing to think about.

GOTCHLING

There's plenty.

AGNES

Nothing pleasant.

GOTCHLING

Unpleasant then.
We need apartments.

(Pause)

We need apartments. Belonging to people who are sympathetic.

AGNES

We who?

GOTCHLING

The Party.

AGNES

The Party's been outlawed.

(Pause.)

GOTCHLING

As I was saying. We need apartments. Way stations to the east. Storage rooms . . .

AGNES

No.

GOTCHLING

Not for storage, then. A way station. There are people hiding . . .

AGNES

No.

GOTCHLING

Agnes.

AGNES

People shouldn't be leaving. They should be staying. Everyone is going. There should be fighting. Who's going to fight? What are people like me supposed to do if people like you just leave?

GOTCHLING

Some of us are staying. Some can't.

AGNES

Are you leaving?

GOTCHLING

I can't say.

AGNES

You are. I knew you would. For God's sake, Annabella, what is going to happen to us?

GOTCHLING

I don't know.

AGNES

And still you recklessly ask me to . . .

GOTCHLING

Not recklessly.

AGNES

It sounds dangerous.

GOTCHLING

It is dangerous.

AGNES

Then I won't do it.

GOTCHLING

The Party needs it.

AGNES

There is no Party! There's no more Party! Wake up! You're a painter, not a politician, you always were a painter so start acting like one!

GOTCHLING

How do I do that, Agnes?

AGNES

Leave me alone!

Gotchling

No. I've never been that kind of a painter.

Art . . . is never enough, it never does enough.

We will be remembered for two things: our communist art, and
our fascist politics.

(Pause.)

Agnes

I don't understand you, Gotchling. You navigate this. You're the
only one. Why is that?

Gotchling

I'm much more intelligent than the rest of you.

Agnes

Then why do you bother with us?

Gotchling

I enjoy feeling superior.

Listen, Agnes.

I am working-class.

And that really does make a difference. I know what's useful,
and what isn't.

I know the price of things,

and I know how to give things up.

I know what it is to struggle—

these tough little lessons

I don't think you people ever learned.

I hold tight, and I do my work.

I make posters for good causes.

Even if they get torn up, I make them,

even though we live in a country

where theory falls silent in the face of fact,

where progress can be reversed overnight,

where the enemy has stolen everything, our own words from us,

I hold tight, and not to my painting . . . not only to that.
Pick any era in history, Agnes.
What is really beautiful about that era?
The way the rich lived?
No.
The way the poor lived?
No.
The dreams of the Left
are always beautiful.
The imagining of a better world
the damnation of the present one.
This faith,
this luminescent anger,
these alone
are worthy of being called human.
These are the Beautiful
that an age produces.
As an artist I am struck to the heart
by these dreams. These visions.
We progress. But at great cost.
How can anyone stand to live
without understanding that much?

Think it over, Agnes. We need the apartment.

(End of scene.)

FROM THE BOOK

(Lights up on Zillah with a Bible.)

ZILLAH

They say that the Book of Revelations is the President's favorite book. This is plausible, once you accept the initial premise, which is that the President knows how to read. It is a great thing, this book. You can try to be reasonable as a clam about evil, but when you get down to La Nitty-Gritty, clams are cold, thick little animals and you just can't find anything more thrilling than this:

(Reading from the Bible) "And He causes all, the rich and the poor, the free and the slave, to receive a mark on their right hand, and none can buy or sell without that mark. The name of the Beast, and the number of that name."

Did you know that *both* Reagan and Margaret Thatcher are afflicted in their right hands with a disease of the manual ligaments called Dupuytren's contracture, which causes the hand to shrivel, gradually assuming, and I quote, "a claw-like appearance." Claw-like.

(Reading again) "Let him who has a mind compute the number of the Beast, for it is the number of a man, and that number is 666."

OK. They say that Hitler used to spell his name A-D-O-L-P-H, and he changed the P-H to an F to make it look less Austrian or more German or something, God knows. Anyway, A-D-O-L-P-H gives you six letters, and H-I-T-L-E-R gives you another six. See where I'm heading? You with me? The problem is that he didn't have a middle name, but not to worry, you can always use F-Ü-H-R-E-R. Et voilà! The name of our own little führer works much better, of course, and with no trouble at all you get the winning number.

(She holds up a poster on which this has been spelled out: R-O-N-A-L-D W-I-L-S-O-N R-E-A-G-A-N)

You know that when he retires he's moving to a big fancy Belair house his friends bought for him, and the address is 666 Mayfair Road. But he had them change the address because, well, he reads the Book.

I didn't work all this out myself. I saw it written on a bathroom stall in Boston. B-O-S-T-O-N. "Do not," we are told, "seal up the words of the pages of this Book, for the time is nigh."

(End of interruption.)

BERLINER SCHNAUSE
(BERLIN LIP)

Slide: MARCH 15, 1933.

(Agnes, Husz and Baz. Baz is standing, wearing an overcoat and cap.)

BAZ

Three days ago I was arrested by the new police. They marched into the Institute after lunch. We were ordered into trucks. Dr. Henni and Dr. Kunz got into black cars. No one knows what happened to Dr. Kunz. He may be dead.

AGNES

Oh my God.

HUSZ

Want a drink?

BAZ

Oh, that would be completely welcome. I have a story.

AGNES

Are you all right? Is the Institute closed?

BAZ

The Institute? Boarded shut, looking very permanently sealed and done for. We were accused of printing pornography and abetting illegal medical practices—abortions. The files were taken. That's bad news. We weren't prepared. Boards on the windows now. Did I say that already?

AGNES

Are you sure you're all right?

BAZ

I cried during the interrogation.

HUSZ

Lots of people do.

BAZ

But it's different when I do it. The mascara runs.

AGNES

Did they . . . do anything to you?

BAZ

One of them slapped me. It was more of a shock than painful. They scream a lot. Then they let us go—half of us, just turned us loose on the street, no explanation, no word about the others.

AGNES

When did they let you go?

BAZ

Two days ago . . . or three? Yes, three.

AGNES

Three days ago? But where have you been? Gotchling's been looking . . .

BAZ

I went to Munich.

AGNES

Why Munich?

BAZ

To kill myself.
Really. I'm very much afraid of them, I have been for years, all police, but these are much more frightening. Being alone with them in a room with a locked door is paralyzing. I looked at the carpet the whole time. I thought, good, they have a carpet, they won't do anything that would get blood on the carpet. When the main one grabbed my face and slapped it I started crying. *(Pause)* I have always been terrified of pain. He said to me, "In the woods outside of Munich, do you know what we are building?" I said no, and he said "A camp. For people like you."
I have a criminal record, I can't get out easily. I expected them to arrest me immediately after letting me go—something they do. So I decided to kill myself.

HUSZ

In Munich.

BAZ

I wanted to go to another city so that none of you would be asked to identify me afterwards. I took the night train. When I got there I bought a revolver and four bullets. Extras. I can't imagine why I thought I'd need extras. Anyway. I wanted to be found by people who aren't particularly frightened or upset by death. Nuns who care for the terminally ill. Better that than in some cafe, ruining some waiter's whole day . . .

HUSZ

You are wonderfully considerate.

BAZ

I try to be. But I felt that killing myself in the midst of a bunch of nuns was probably a much more serious sin than doing it discreetly in a secular location. So I went to the park.

AGNES

And . . . ?

BAZ

Agnes, I met a remarkably attractive young Silesian there. I was exhausted. Fatigue makes me easy to arouse . . .

HUSZ

So you did it in the bushes.

BAZ

Husz, you are a man of the world.

HUSZ

After which you decided not to die.

BAZ

I realized after my Silesian friend left that it had been nearly a week since my last orgasm. Too much pent-up energy. The result: depression. Add to it the nightmare of the last few days—suicide. One brisk interlude with a pliable friend and my desire to live returned to me in all its hot, tainted glory.

AGNES

And so you came home?

BAZ

No. There's more. The best part.

AGNES

More?

BAZ

Well, here I am in Munich with a little money, a loaded gun, and a whole day to kill before the night train to Berlin. What to do?

AGNES

Hang around the bushes.

BAZ

No, Agnes. Once a day, every day, not too seldom, not too often, balance is everything. I went to the cinema. And you are absolutely not going to believe what happened.

HUSZ

You saw a film.

BAZ

Yes, of course, but not only that. It was a Dietrich film. And there was hardly anyone there, it being early in the day, just me and some old people and some war vets. When all of a sudden into the theatre marches a squadron of brownshirts and guess who else?

HUSZ

Ummm . . . Adolf Hitler.

BAZ

Right.

(There is a pause.)

AGNES

You're making this up.

BAZ

I am not. It was him. In a slouch hat and a trench coat. And someone else with him, a man I didn't recognize.

HUSZ

I don't believe this.

BAZ

Well I told you you wouldn't but it's perfectly true. Hitler. And he sat down three rows in front of me. The S.A. sat in back of him but I had a clear view of the back of his head. I could see the oil in his hair.

AGNES

Oh my God.

BAZ

Just what I said.

The film got going and I was thinking to myself, "Life plays funny tricks. Here we are, watching a Dietrich film: ten pensioners, six war-cripples, Adolf Hitler and me, a homosexual Sunday anarchist with a loaded gun in his pocket."

(He shapes the gun with his fingers, aims carefully, and makes a soft "bang")

So I left.

HUSZ

You what?

BAZ

I left.

(Another pause.)

HUSZ

Is this true?

BAZ

Yes, it is.

HUSZ

It's true? Adolf Hitler?

BAZ

Yes.

Husz

And you left?

Baz

I left.

(Husz jumps up, runs over to Baz, grabs him by the shirt front and begins shaking him furiously.)

Husz

WHY DIDN'T YOU SHOOT? YOU HAD A GUN! YOU FUCKING IDIOT! WHY DIDN'T YOU SHOOT!

(Agnes grabs Husz, who shoves Baz away and storms to the opposite side of the room.)

Agnes

Husz! Please, stop yelling, what are you saying, he . . .

Husz

What am I saying? What am I saying? Why didn't he shoot? *I* would have shot! Why? *(Running back to Baz but not touching him)* WHAT IS THE MATTER WITH YOU?

Baz

Because, Husz.
Because they would have shot me.

Agnes

Baz, you're making all of this up.

Baz

No. I couldn't get my hand to move, to even begin to move towards the pocket that had the gun. Because I might have killed him, but they would certainly have killed me. And I don't want to die.

Husz

Adolf Hitler!

Baz

I do not want to die.

(Husz turns his back on Baz. There is a pause.)

Baz

A friend is arranging a phony passport and visa. They'll be ready in six days. I'm leaving. That's what I came to tell you. I'm leaving.

Slide: MARCH 15, 1933.
Slide: OPENING CEREMONIES
Slide: DACHAU CONCENTRATION CAMP.

(End of scene.)

Slide: MAY 1–JUNE 22, 1933.
Slide: THE TRANSITION TO FASCISM
Slide: GATHERS INCREDIBLE SPEED.
Slide: THE 150-YEAR-OLD GERMAN LABOR MOVEMENT
Slide: VANISHES OVERNIGHT
Slide: WITH ALMOST NO RESISTANCE.
Slide: THE SOCIAL-DEMOCRATIC PARTY IS OUTLAWED.
Slide: ALL MEANINGFUL AUTHORITY IS CONCENTRATED
Slide: IN THE HANDS OF THE CHANCELLOR.
Slide: IF THE SYSTEM IS NOT IN FACT COMPLETE & TOTAL,
Slide: THE ILLUSION OF TOTALITY IS ENOUGH.
Slide: THE NAZIS CONTROL NOT ONLY THE FUTURE
Slide: BUT THE PAST AS WELL.
Slide: CENTURIES OF PROGRESS SEEM
Slide: NEVER TO HAVE TAKEN PLACE.

SEVENTH INTERRUPTION

EPITAPH

(Lights up on Zillah at her table and Agnes in her room.)

ZILLAH

Sometimes at nights now I hear her moving around, sort of shuffling, patching cracks, moving things, looking for some lost object.

(Agnes moves to the cupboard, opens drawers, looks out the window.)

ZILLAH

Heavy steps, hardly the heart to move her feet. I ask her what her name was.

(Agnes stops moving, looks around the room, sensing something.)

ZILLAH

She stops moving, so I know she hears me. No answer. I ask her how she died.

(Agnes stops moving completely, frightened.)

ZILLAH

An air raid? In the camps? Because I know she died then, unhappy. Again, she doesn't move, and she hasn't answered me yet but when she does I already know what she'll say: "Not in the camps, and not in the war, but at home, in front of a cozy fire, I died of a broken heart."

(Agnes gasps.)

AGNES

Hello? Hello? Who's . . .
Oh dear God I need to sleep.
(She flees the room)

(End of interruption.)

SCENE NINETEEN

DER WILDGEWORDENE KLEINBÜRGER (THE PETIT-BOURGEOIS RUN AMOK)

Slide: MAY 1, 1933.

(The apartment is dark. Die Alte staggers drunkenly about the room, clutching a bottle. She turns on the radio. It warms up, but plays nothing but static. She bangs violently on the table, three times.)

DIE ALTE

(Shouts)
So it's Ho! for the man with the iron nails
And the slippery tongue so black.
With his foul breath and his hands, bang bang,
All a-sweat on the damp dirty bed, bang bang,
As he pulls at your hair, and he claws at your back,
And he tickles your neck and your crack, bang bang,
And he tickles your neck and your crack.

(Agnes rushes in during this.)

AGNES

This has got to end! *What do you want here?*

DIE ALTE

I had a black pillow once . . .

AGNES

(Heading back to the bedroom) I can't listen to this anymore!

DIE ALTE

I HAD A BLACK PILLOW ONCE ON MY BED AND I HAD
HORRIBLE DREAMS!

(Agnes is listening.)

DIE ALTE

Horrible, every night. It's the black pillow, they'd warn me, you
can't sleep peacefully with your head resting on that. But I loved
that pillow. I'd have thrown the whole bed out before I'd throw
that black pillow away. I held on to it for years.

AGNES

And the dreams?

DIE ALTE

Every night for years.

AGNES

What happened?

DIE ALTE

I wound up all alone.

(Small pause.)

AGNES

I'm afraid of you.

DIE ALTE

You look green.
(She holds her bottle towards Agnes)
I'd offer you some but it's mine. Beer. *German* beer. Not vodka
like you and your Bolshevik friends drink.

(Small pause.)

AGNES

My friends aren't . . .

DIE ALTE

(Suddenly in a rage) BOLSHEVIK! BOLSHEVIK! FUCKING
BOLSHEVIK PIGS, ALL OF YOU! This nest; I know! You'll be
reported . . .

(Agnes grabs a broom which is standing nearby.)

DIE ALTE

If you strike me with that I promise you you'll wish you hadn't.

AGNES

(Putting the broom down) Who are you?

DIE ALTE

A bad dream.

AGNES

Get out!

DIE ALTE

I live here!

AGNES

This is my apartment!

DIE ALTE

Mine!

AGNES

Mine! You have no right to be here!

DIE ALTE

I'm hungry, do you have any . . .

(Agnes grabs the old woman and begins to drag her towards the door. Die Alte suddenly becomes very strong, and the two women begin to struggle.)

AGNES

Let go of me let go . . .

(Die Alte wraps Agnes in a fierce embrace, which transforms as Agnes stops struggling into a tender, enveloping hug. Die Alte rocks Agnes in her arms.)

DIE ALTE

(Softly) There there there there . . .
Kicking and fighting. How silly it is. Feel better now?

AGNES

(Softly) Yes. Better. Please let go.

DIE ALTE

(Whispers) Time is all that separates you from me.

(The radio static flares up and then begins to play Bach's Unaccompanied Violin Sonata in G minor.)

DIE ALTE

Some dance. Nice music.
It's bad to be too much alone.

(End of scene.)

AN ACID
MORNING LIGHT

Slide: MAY 2, 1933.
Slide: WITH MINIMAL RESISTANCE
Slide: GERMAN TRADE UNIONS ARE ABOLISHED.

(The next morning. Husz is in a chair, bloody face, clothes torn. Paulinka is pouring herself a stiff drink. Agnes stares at Husz.)

HUSZ

You see, there was a little riot . . .

PAULINKA

At the Studio.

HUSZ

Paulinka is a hero!

PAULINKA

Shut up, Husz.

Husz

They closed down the electricians union. Some of the electricians didn't understand that. It got very ugly and everyone left . . .

Agnes

But you didn't.

Husz

LEAVE?! I WANTED TO *FILM* IT! And I wanted to hit someone! A whole gaggle of fascists surrounded me in a stairwell and they had their little sticks at the ready . . .

Paulinka

They nearly killed him.

Husz

Nearly. They were interrupted by one of Germany's minor celebrities . . .

Paulinka

Minor? I resent that!

Husz

Crying "Leave that man alone!" She marched up out of nowhere, goes to the biggest ugliest one, says "Klaus! This is beneath you!" and she slaps him. Pow! He drops his little stick, rubs his face, and says "My name isn't Klaus." And then he looks at the other Nazis, and they walked away, completely ashamed of themselves.

Paulinka

The performance of my career. Wasted on a crazed Hungarian and three Nazi thugs.

Husz

Five.

Paulinka

Three, Husz. Three. Five and I would have pretended not to know you.

AGNES

(Having a hard time piecing this story together, to Paulinka) "Klaus, this is beneath you"?

PAULINKA

A line from the film I'm doing. Just popped out. The slap too. If I hadn't been drugged all morning I'd never have done it.
(To Husz) They're going to come after you for this. God help you. I have to go.

HUSZ

Of course you're terrified. It makes sense to be terrified. But to stand up to the terror! Resistance! That is a great thing.

PAULINKA

(A beat, then) I was there, Husz, at the Studio to tell Special Propaganda Chief Otto Von Something-or-Other that I would be interested, yes, in accepting his offer of continued employment within the film industries of the Third Reich.
And you distracted me. So shit on you and your stupid moral dilemmas. *(Slight pause)* Oh, and here. *(She takes a big kitchen knife out of her purse and stabs it into the table top)* This is yours.
(She leaves, slamming the door)

HUSZ

Germans . . . are full of surprises.

AGNES

(Looking at knife) I don't understand this . . .

HUSZ

You don't? Really? It's a butcher knife. I carry it around with me these days, hoping I'll run into someone . . . with ideological differences, and I'll make him see the point, as it were.

AGNES

I don't want that thing in my house. I don't want you here with that.

Husz

History repeats itself, see, first as tragedy, then as farce. When I was young . . .

Agnes

I don't want you here!

(Pause. He looks at her.)

Husz

Then I'll leave.

Agnes

Go!

(Husz stands, pulls the knife out of the table top so roughly it splinters the wood.)

Agnes

My table! You bastard! Get out! Go!

(Husz starts to limp to the door, then sits heavily on the floor, unable to walk.)

Agnes

Go! Go! Go!

Husz

I can't.

(Pause. Then Agnes sits on the floor as well. End of scene.)

LOVE SCENE
WITHOUT...

Slide: MAY 2, 1933. LATE.

(Husz is seated, without a shirt, linen wrapped around his ribs. Agnes is sweeping.)

Husz

It will not be hard to leave Berlin.
You can't imagine how much I miss Hungary. You can't imagine how much I hate German cooking. You can't imagine what it's cost me to be a castaway here, making German films, churning out the kind of bad dreams a drug addict or a criminal lunatic has before he wakes up and does something terrible.

AGNES

Husz . . .

Husz

Sssshhh.

Justice . . . is vanishing. Like all the air in the earth's atmosphere getting used up, like life's blood running freely on the ground, pouring from a wound too big to stop up; you watch it spill, watching yourself die. Justice precedes beauty. Without justice, beauty is impossible, an obscenity. And when beauty has gone, what does a cameraman do with his eye?

AGNES

I think we should go to the hospital.

HUSZ

Get me my coat, I have something for you.

(Agnes gets his coat.)

HUSZ

(Producing two packets of official-looking documents) There. One for me, one . . .

(He hands Agnes a packet. She looks at it, places it on the table.)

AGNES

I didn't apply for a visa.

HUSZ

Counterfeit of course, but eminently serviceable. I have cousins in Chicago. There's a boat from Denmark, five days from today. I want you to come with me.

AGNES

I want you to go to a doctor.

HUSZ

When I lost my eye in 1919, it was the doctor who treated it who turned me in.

AGNES

You're hurt.

HUSZ

You have done extraordinary things with this bed-linen bandage. And I seem to be able to walk.

AGNES

The foot is broken.

HUSZ

No, I don't think so. Just very badly bruised.

AGNES

(Softly) I can't go, Husz.

HUSZ

Why not?

AGNES

I don't speak English. I can't function in strange places. It took me years to get a contract, what kind of work would I do in Chicago? Traveling upsets me. Really. I can't move. I can't move. I'm sorry. Later, maybe . . .

HUSZ

This is no time, Agnes, for alliances that aren't portable.

AGNES

Stay.

HUSZ

I can't.

(Pause.)

AGNES

Leave then. Throw your life away. But don't expect to find anything waiting for you when you come back.

Husz

Goodbye, dear heart. I promise to write.

(He embraces Agnes, tries to kiss her. She pushes him away.)

Husz

It will not be hard to leave Berlin. But it will be very hard to leave you.

(End of scene.)

HANDS

Slide: MAY 3, 1933.

(Agnes is sitting alone at the table. She picks up the visa Husz has left behind. She tears it in half.)

AGNES

(Holding up her right hand)
With this hand
I

hold water,
stir the soup,
crack walnuts,
turn keys,
scratch,
move, divide,

replace,
light the light,
write postcards,
pay,
receive payment,
grasp,
fill out a ballot, seal it,
take up a knife,
make a cut.
The practical hand,
this hand,
its veins, nerves, tissue
and bones
Five fingers has this hand.
With five I can . . .
(Holding up her left hand)
Now this hand.
With this hand,
weak claw, I
shred shadows,
brush dust,
drop glass, let go,
sense changes in the air by
the subcutaneous twingings,
the shy retirement of heat
to cool inner safety;
this hand to make
a frail moon-cup
protective patch
over the weak eye,
the eye that cannot bear to see.
Five fingers has this hand.
With five I can . . .

(Holds up right hand) And this is the hand that betrays me.
(Holds up left hand) And this is the hand that holds my life.

(End of scene.)

Slide: MAY 10, 1933.
Slide: HITLER DECLARES HIS INTENTION
Slide: TO "ABOLISH CLASS WAR."
Slide: LATER THAT NIGHT
Slide: THE FIRST PUBLIC BOOK BURNINGS ARE HELD.

REVELATIONS AND FAREWELLS

Slide: JUNE 22, 1933.

(Agnes stands near the window, looking out. Paulinka is dressed for travel. Baz is in a chair, his coat and valise nearby.)

PAULINKA

The train ride to Moscow will take three days. The trip to Hollywood would have taken a month. So I decided to go to Russia.
Well, not really. The Americans found out about my old KPD membership.

BAZ

Remarkable.

PAULINKA

What kind of a world is it where Husz moves to America and I wind up in the USSR? Doesn't that seem . . . backwards or something?

BAZ

Don't talk about Husz when you get to Moscow. Don't say you knew him. Stay out of politics.

PAULINKA

Easy for me to do.

There was this woman in wardrobe who used to fold a KPD leaflet very carefully and slip it into the pocket of my costume on the sly. Every once in a while. Then she'd wait for me to find it, and when I did she'd be watching, and she'd wink at me. I hated her. Last week, I guess someone informed on her; they came for her at the Studio. She screamed. But . . .

That was it for me. I faked a nervous breakdown, or maybe I didn't fake it, who knows. And so on. The end.

You're being ominously quiet, Agnes. You could at least wish me a pleasant voyage east.

(Pause. Agnes looks at Paulinka, then out the window again.)

BAZ

The winters in Russia have a nasty reputation.

PAULINKA

I packed my fur. And I expect a warm welcome in Moscow. I, too, have a reputation.

It isn't so terrible. They do make the best films.

BAZ

Not recently.

PAULINKA

Don't be so morbid, Baz. Put a good face on it.

BAZ

Hard to do.

PAULINKA

Apparently. Not for me. Frightening, isn't it? What an actor does? Assume the mantle of truth, of courage, of moral conviction, and wear it convincingly, no matter what sort of chaotic mess there is inside.

Agnes, you have to say something.

AGNES

You . . . are going to miss your train.
I wish you'd go now. Please go.

(Little pause. Paulinka leaves.)

AGNES

See? You'd think, when a person goes, a whole person just goes away, it would leave a hole, some empty place behind, that's what I thought, I imagined that, but . . . it doesn't. Everyone's going but it isn't like the world has gotten emptier, just much smaller. It contracts, the empty places . . . collapse.
Goodbye.

BAZ

Plans? What are you . . .

AGNES

Sssshhhh. Goodbye. Please.

BAZ

Do you remember ten years ago, Agnes?
One red word and a streetful of people would come running.

The Revolution.
When I was sixteen, in Leipzig, I joined
a band of young people——we went
off to the mountains,
read Wedekind and Whitman the American,
and Schubert and Mahler the Jew,
worshipped the sun, made a god of nature,
experimented with each other
in all sorts of ways, and then . . .
We got crazy, we got pregnant, we
discovered urges we wished we'd left alone.
Everyone fled back to Leipzig, back
to upholstered furniture, marriage,
heterosexuality, each
to his or her own prison.
We were too young and too frightened
to see how close we'd come to something
truly free;
knocked on the gates of the Divinity,
only to retreat in terror.
(He stands to leave)
Today I saw a platoon of children,
younger than we were,
marching to the mountains.
As organized as ants. They wear uniforms.
They plan experiments of a different kind.
They'll dream blood-dreams
of goats rutting and lions killing,
and they'll sing songs about racial purity.
Their revolution, I think, will succeed.
They'd be the future except
they stand as a guarantee

that no future exists.
Only a long, long nightfall,
and then a permanent good-night.

Good night. Paris awaits.
(He reaches in his pocket, takes out an orange, places it on the table)
Weather this, Agnes. And keep the door locked. *(Exits)*

(End of scene.)

Slide: JULY 14–17, 1933.
Slide: ALL LEGISLATIVE AND POLITICAL WORK
Slide: NECESSARY FOR THE ESTABLISHMENT
Slide: OF THE THIRD REICH HAS BEEN COMPLETED.
Slide: THE FASCIST MACHINERY CREATED IN SIX MONTHS
Slide: WOULD FUNCTION EFFICIENTLY
Slide: FOR THE NEXT THIRTEEN YEARS.

ALL THAT WAS FAT AND BRIGHT IS PERISHED FROM YOU

(Gotchling and Agnes.)

AGNES

What do you want?

GOTCHLING

That's quite a welcome.

AGNES

I haven't seen you for months. You must want something. I thought you'd gone for good.

GOTCHLING

I have, officially.

AGNES

Officially where?

GOTCHLING

Officially Switzerland.

AGNES

And really where?

GOTCHLING

Switzerland.

AGNES

Lie.

GOTCHLING

You don't want the truth.

AGNES

Lie.

GOTCHLING

It doesn't matter. I need your help. The apartment . . .

AGNES

I knew it. The answer's no.

GOTCHLING

There's no one else. You have to.

AGNES

I do not. You can't make me risk my life. Risk your own.

GOTCHLING

I am.

AGNES

Good for you. How wonderful. I refuse this honor.

GOTCHLING

Tell you what. We'll make a deal.
(No answer)
You can't save yourself, Agnes. If you make it, you make it, but
only because you're lucky.

AGNES

I don't know what you're talking about.

GOTCHLING

You will.

If you say no to this, Agnes, you're dead to me. And we both need desperately to keep at least some part of you alive. Say yes, and I promise to carry you with me, the part of you that's dying now. I can do that, I'm stronger than you. Say yes, and I will take your heart and fold it up in mine, and protect it with my life. And some day I may be able to bring it back to you.

You're very fond of regrets, Agnes, but the time for regretting is gone. I need very much to be proud of you.

AGNES

If I get arrested, Annabella Gotchling, I swear to God I will never forgive you.

GOTCHLING

Three days from now, around six in the evening. Expect her. She says she knows you. Her name is Rosa. *(Exits)*

(End of scene.)

EIGHTH INTERRUPTION

LULLABY

(Lights up on Zillah.)

ZILLAH

There's a terror that skips
over the mind and out the throat

faster than thinking:
Revelation: We
are in danger.
It catches us by surprise,
on sweet evenings
when we're most thoroughly
at home,
and says look
for the cracks
where the seams don't meet,
look where the walls
have moved slightly apart,
try to see, stay awake,
there isn't time for sleeping.
Hören? Kannst du mich hören?
Before the sky and the ground
slam shut. . . . Now.

(End of interruption.)

THE GREEN FRONT

(There is a soft knock at the door. The knock again. Agnes goes quickly to the door, opens it a crack, then lets Rosa Malek in.)

AGNES

No one saw you.

MALEK

No.

AGNES

How can you tell? There are so many doorways and alleys and windows.

MALEK

I don't think anyone saw me.

AGNES

You don't *think*? Oh God in heaven.

MALEK

You've got to calm down. What if someone saw me? I'm not wearing a red beret and a sign saying "escaping communist."

AGNES

But later, when they come looking—I shouldn't have done this, I really shouldn't. It's no joke. Goddamned Annabella. They'll find out. The hateful people in this building. They watch everything. They get money for informing. Calm, calm, I need a drink. Do you want a drink?

MALEK

Yes, please.

(Agnes pours two glasses and gives one to Malek. They both sit.)

AGNES

But you can't stay here long.

MALEK

Just till morning.

AGNES

Morning. Then you've got to leave. And don't give this address to anyone else.

MALEK

No.

(Pause.)

AGNES

(Calmer) Where are you going? After here?

MALEK

I can't say.

AGNES

No, well, no, that's . . . that makes sense. I wouldn't actually want to know. But . . . you'll still be . . . working.

MALEK

I really can't talk about that.

AGNES

No. Please. I'm sorry. You probably think I'm a spy. I . . . I haven't changed that much.
I just need to know that you'll be working. You and Gotchling. You'll keep doing what needs to be done, underground, I couldn't, I'm not really worth much, I suppose . . . the fear is too great, it makes me stupid, but. . . . It still matters to me.

MALEK

I know it does, Agnes.

AGNES

And this will pass. Months, not years.

MALEK

There are people working, Agnes, and it will pass. But it could be years.

AGNES

Oh no, not years, I don't think so.
I'm afraid of living alone here, that something will happen to me. Stupid of me telling you this, you have such real things to be frightened of but . . . I'm lonely. And years frightens me. I ought to do something to help but I'm simply not able. The arrests. Every day they execute . . .

MALEK

This is important. What you've done for me.

AGNES

(Suddenly angry) This is nothing. Don't coddle me. This is shit. I think we should go to sleep *(She gets up and goes toward the bedroom)*

MALEK

Agnes.

(Agnes stops but does not look at Malek.)

MALEK

On the border, in Karlsbad, there's a house: 30 Herze Street. Memorize the address, don't write it down. 30 Herze, like the mountains. The front of the house is in Germany. The back of the house is in Czechoslovakia. The people who live there are . . . friends of ours, and the Nazis don't know about it yet—the system is full of little holes like this. Go there by train, at night, if it gets bad here; knock on the door and tell them you're looking for the Green Front. They'll take you to the back door, and you're out.

If you need to. Ask for the way to the Green Front. The borders are full of holes.

(Agnes walks slowly to the bedroom without looking back.)

AGNES

Please be gone by morning.
(She closes the bedroom door)

(End of scene.)

Slide: OCTOBER 14, 1933

Slide: GERMANY WITHDRAWS FROM DISARMAMENT TALKS

Slide: AND FROM THE LEAGUE OF NATIONS.

Slide: NOVEMBER 12, 1933

Slide: REICHSTAG ELECTIONS AND A NATIONAL PLEBISCITE.

Slide: A 95% POPULAR VOTE OF CONSENT.

EPILOGUE

*(Agnes, alone at the kitchen table. She has an orange, which she push-
es, causing it to roll off the table and across the floor. Die Alte enters
through the bedroom door, picks up the orange and begins to peel and
eat it. Zillah watches.)*

AGNES

I live in a modern flat.
On one side lives nightmare,
on the other despair.
Above me, exhaustion,
below me, a man
with the pale face
and red handsof a strangler.

DIE ALTE

I can eat anywhere. I remember
the thick smoke rising from the ruins of home,
black plumes in an ash-white sky,
the sun transformed
into a nickel-plated dot
no bigger than a groschen. It seemed
to race through the clouds—
or was that the moon? No.
The sun. The moon
was huge and rusted
like an infected eye.
It moved slowly, and the nights were black.
Rats looked for bodies under the rubble,
so corpses had to be torched right in the street:
a piteous sight.
The planes came back
every day
to bomb the craters they'd created
only the day before.
The water was oily
and full of typhus.
Everyone was patchy,
delirious, diseased,
and waiting for the end . . .

AGNES

When God is good
The hours go,
But the world rolls on,
Tumbrel-slow,

And the driver sings
A gallows song:
"The end is quick.
The way is long."
I fear the end
I fear the way
I fear the wind
Will make me stray
Much farther than
I want to stray
Far from my home
Bright room called day;
past where deliverance or hope
can find me.

Die Alte

But through it all
I never lost my appetite,
and never ceased to look for food,
just like the rats.
I ate while the bombs fell,
ate while the bodies burned,
ate at the funerals, hurried and undignified,
of people I had loved . . .
Ate
through days of pain
and nights of terror;
with cracked teeth
and split lips
I kept eating, digesting,
and looking for meals.

When they rounded us up,
and brought us to the camps,

and showed us the mass graves and said
"You
are responsible for these."
I was thinking, "I
wasn't here,
didn't know,
didn't want to know,
never pulled a trigger,
never pulled a switch,
feel nothing for these beds
of sleepers, deep asleep,
but only
look at how thin they are,
and when they let us return to Munich
I wonder what I'll find for dinner."

(The room begins to grow dark.)

ZILLAH

Now.
Before the sky and the ground slam shut.
The borders are full of holes.

AGNES

Clubfoot.
Smell of sulphur.
Yellow dog.
No shadow.

Welcome to Germany.

END OF PLAY

ZILLAH INTERRUPTIONS, NEW YORK SHAKESPEARE FESTIVAL VERSION

For the New York Shakespeare Festival production, Zillah had moved to Berlin, in the recently reunified Germany; she was living in Agnes's apartment, forty years later, and had picked up a young German, Roland (played by the actor playing Traum). Roland is in his twenties, born in East Germany back when there was such a thing. He's now hanging out in what was formerly West Berlin. He speaks no English.

This monologue began the play. It is the first part of the Prologue; the Berlin scene followed after.

PROLOGUE

EVENING MEAL IN A WINDSTORM

(The empty apartment, 1990: repeated slides of a huge crowd rallying in support of Hitler, everyone giving the fascist salute. With each slide the people in the crowd draw nearer, till finally we fix on a single figure, a woman who isn't saluting. Zillah enters with a suitcase in hand. She is carrying a large book: a photo history of the Third Reich. She shows its open pages to the audience.)

ZILLAH

Ich bin eine Berliner.
Oh well not really.
Ich nicht eine Berliner, ich bin actually
eine Long Islander.
Ich bin Zillah Katz, nach Great Neck.
And that's all the German I know.

I don't know about you but for me,
the way I remember is usually in fact
a way of forgetting. Memory easily

becomes memorial: a blank stone marker
denoting: Event—
a tombstone under which
the bodies are buried, out of sight,
under which
the warning voice of what happened
is silenced.
Time now to remember, to re-call:
dismantle the memorial, disinter
the dead:

To call into the Now
other people, not my own;
an other city, not my own, an other people, not mine.
History. As I conjure it.
From out of too many nights spent
reading and dreaming,
from out of a book,
from out of a crowd:
I find
one lonely
familiar
other face . . .
Now.

The First Interruption was positioned between Scenes 2 and 3.

FIRST INTERRUPTION

BERLIN 1990: HYSTERIA

(Zillah and Roland are in the apartment. Zillah talks mostly to the audience, occasionally or when indicated to Roland, who listens to her with uncomprehending friendly fascination.)

ZILLAH

Berlin.

When I told my parents I was leaving New York and moving to Berlin they reacted pretty much like I thought they would:

(She screams, she sobs)

So why did I tell them? Because I always tell them everything I do. Because I am Basically Bourgeois.

Take sleep, for instance: sleep is essentially a bourgeois convention, right? I mean no one who's looking open-eyed at all the awfulness there is everywhere would want to or in fact be able to sleep, any decent person should be too busy being hysterical to sleep, and when I was struck by the full realization of this, of what sleep really is, which happened at about 3:27 a.m. Election Night 1980, I decided to break the chains of my middle-class epistemological predispositions, break the chains of Reason and Common Sense, and not sleep anymore, but because I am not a true hysteric, but rather a hysterical rationalist—which is not the same thing, it's a sort of self-canceling term—I knew that my insomnia jag, going on its tenth year now thank you very much, would need a pharmaceutical boost to supplement the adrenaline rush I couldn't come by honestly through hysterical terror and I figured: I live in the East Village: speed. Right? But I took No-Doz instead and why? Because speed is drugs and it would upset my mother. Basically bourgeois. I read too much for one thing, I mean people who have attained a really appropriate level of Panic in the face of for instance the nine hundredth reelection of Jesse Helms—these true hysterics don't read much I imagine because well they can't sit still for that long. I read. This suitcase? No clothes: books. I am not a camera; I would like to be a camera; or maybe something more I don't know *participatory* than a camera even but instead I am the Zombie Graduate Student of the Living Dead. Except that I am nowhere matriculated. At large. In Berlin.

(To Roland) Lenny Bernsteen—*stein*, was just in town conducting the Ninth, did you catch it, over by the Wall? Beethoven? Sprechen Sie Beethoven?

ROLAND
Beethoven, ja. Er ist in der Stadt geboren, in der ich geboren wurde. [Beethoven sure, he was born in the same city I was.]

ZILLAH
It was a big celebration in honor of the End of History and the end of Ideology and Reunification and all that, and Lenny did the Ninth only they changed the words of the Chorus: not Freude anymore: Freiheit.

ROLAND
Freiheit. Super. [Freedom. Super.]

ZILLAH
My German sucks but I read *Time* magazine: Not Joy. Freedom. Me, I would rather have Freude. Freiheit's just another word for nothing left to lose.
Lenny Lenny Lenny, oh what is the world coming to? *Is* this the end of History? And *what* am I *doing* here? In Berlin!

ROLAND

Ich denke, Beethoven ist da geboren. Jedenfalls, ich bin es. Weisst du wo Leipzig ist? [I think Beethoven was born there. Anyway, I was. Do you know where Leipzig is?]

ZILLAH

What?

ROLAND

Ich bin total doof. Ich habe nie Englisch lernen können. Französisch auch nicht. [I'm a total moron. I could never learn English. French either.]

ZILLAH

I'm sorry I don't . . .
We have a communications problem.

(End of interruption.)

The Second Interruption was positioned between Scenes 8 and 9.

SECOND INTERRUPTION

BERLIN 1990: HISTORY

(Zillah and Roland. Books everywhere. Roland is looking at the pictures.)

ZILLAH

What did your daddy do in the War?

ROLAND

Vielleicht sollen wir 'was essen gehen. Indisch? [Maybe we should go for food. Indian?]

ZILLAH

I've always wanted to ask a German that. In New York I met plenty of Germans but they all spoke English so I never had the nerve; you I can ask and you won't be offended or guilty or anything because you won't understand the question and I don't understand the answer. It's perfect.

ROLAND

Ich bin noch jungfräulich. Ausserdem, bin ich Sozialist, ich bin nicht nach dem Westen gefahren, um Tennisschuhe zukaufen, aber ich wurde schon gern mal bumsen. [I'm still a virgin. Anyway, I'm a socialist, I didn't come to the West to buy tennis shoes, but I would like to get laid.]

ZILLAH

Wow. This city: this language: History, right? Even him, I have no idea who this guy is, I picked him up in some bar my first night here, I mean like don't you ever go home or anything? All right so he's a little young to be historical but still he looks like *them*, like *they* looked back then, in all those black-and-white photos they took of themselves. . . . Or this apartment—I knew when I got here I didn't want one of those economic miracle aluminum/ linoleum events, I wanted this: a squat nineteenth-century job that made it through the bombings. It's tonic, all this historical grit: History: it smells like Garbage. Wonderful.

ROLAND

Ich glaube, ich sollte dich warnen, ich bin vielleicht bisexuel. Ich fühle mich schwindlig. [I think I should warn you, I may be bisexual. I feel dizzy.]

ZILLAH

Me? Oh I just couldn't hack it back in the United States of Amnesia. The last decade was too hard for a history junkie like myself—The Decade of the Great Commmunicator. Your Great Communicator spoke and created a whole false history, ours spoke and History basically came down with arteriosclerosis; from the Triumph of the Will to the Triumph of the Brain-Dead—from National Socialism to National Senility. Eight years of watching him try to remember his lines: it was our national cliffhanger: Is he finally going to go totally blank in front of an audience of three-point-six billion people and just stand there waggling his head, you know the way he does, *(She does it)* "Shake up those neurons, something'll come." And *this* is a Great Communicator? *YES!* Because what he was communicating to a nation that wanted desperately to go to sleep and get lost in dreams because reality was becoming too damn ugly was: "FORGET EVERYTHING, FOLKS." Because what Reagan communicated is that you can be even more divorced from History and Reality and Language than he was from Jane Wyman and STILL BE THE MOST POWERFUL MAN ON EARTH!

ROLAND

Reagan?

ZILLAH

Reagan.

ROLAND

(Doing Reagan with a thick German accent) "Mister Gorbachev, tear down this wall!" Ich hab's im Fernsehen gesehen. [I saw it on TV.]

ZILLAH

And after the twenty-five people who bothered to vote in 1988 voted for the Kennebunkport Katastrophe and the party that bought you Iran Contra, I said to myself nuts to this, I need to reconnect with History, I need to find some ghosts, I need to go someplace so haunted there's no way to hide the haunts—back to the basics, I said to myself, back to the bone. Back, in point of fact, to Berlin.

(End of interruption.)

The Third Interruption was positioned between Scenes 12 and 13.

THIRD INTERRUPTION

BERLIN 1990: THE POLITICS OF PARANOIA

(Roland is asleep on the floor.)

ZILLAH

(In a soft voice) Sssshhh. Don't wake him up. He got worn out. We were having German lessons. Listen:

"Das Massengrab." Mass grave.

"Die Zeit war sehr schlimm." Times were bad.

"Millionen von Menschen waren tot." Millions of people were dead.

People try to be so fussy and particular when they look at politics, but what I think an understanding of the second half of the twentieth century calls for is not caution and circumspection but moral exuberance. Overstatement is your friend: use it. Take Evil: The problem is that we have a standard of what Evil is, Hitler, the Holocaust—THE standard of absolute evil, and why? Because it's so clear. So stark. Most other instances of evil are more veiled, hidden, the trails are better covered, they're harder to see. So as Standards of Evil go, this is more than adequate. But then everyone gets frantic as soon as you try to use the standard, *nothing* compares, *nothing* resembles—and the standard becomes unusable and *nothing* qualifies as Evil with a capital E. I mean how much of a Nazi do you have to be to qualify for membership? Is a twenty-five-percent Nazi a Nazi or not? Ask yourselves this: it's 1942; the Goerings are having an intimate soiree; if he got an invitation, would Pat Buchanan feel out of place? Out of place? Are you *kidding*? Pig *heaven*, dust off the old tuxedo, kisses to Eva and Adolf. I mean like a certain ex-actor-turned-President who shall go nameless sat idly and I do mean *idly* by and watched tens of thousands die of a plague and he couldn't even bother to say he felt *bad* about it, much less try to help but still be reasonable why should you expect the President of the United States to be anything other than a complete moral reprobate? I mean do you have to pile up some magic number of bodies before you hit the jackpot and rate a comparison to you-know-who? Why isn't *one* body enough? Or fifty? Or just the *likelihood*, the *intention* enough, like is this some sort of Olympic event, handicapping Holocausts, and if it is an Olympic event I hope someone's got a Bronze Medal set aside for George Bush, Mr. How're-my-ratings?, because kinder gentler America is just about ready any second now to weigh in with a little mass murder of our own devising. I mean I ask you—how come the only people who ever say "Evil" anymore are southern cracker televangelists with radioactive blue eyeshadow? No, none of these bastards *look* like Hitler, they never will, not exactly, but I say as long as they look like they're playing in Mr. Hitler's Neighborhood we got no reason to relax.

(Roland stirs in his sleep.)

ZILLAH

I never relax. Moral exuberance. Hallucination, vision, revelation, paranoia, gut-flutters in the night—the internal intestinal night bats, their panicky leathery wings—that's my common sense. I pay attention to that.

Don't put too much stock in a good night's sleep. During times of reactionary backlash, the only people sleeping soundly are the guys who're giving the rest of us bad dreams. So eat something indigestible before you go to bed, and listen to your nightmares.

(End of interruption.)

The song "Memories of You" was eliminated in the NYSF production; Part Two began with Scene 14.

The Fourth Interruption was positioned between Scenes 14 and 15, where the Fifth Interruption is in the current version.

FOURTH INTERRUPTION

BERLIN 1990: NIGHT BATS

ZILLAH

Spooky.

Recently when I have succumbed to sleep, my dreams are invaded by a woman dressed in a frumpy hat and coat—and for a change it's not Mom. This woman—I think she came from a book I read—a photograph of a huge crowd, thousands of people, a rally, everyone, and I mean *everyone* giving the fascist salute. But there she is, right in the middle of all these ecstatic people waving their hands, and she isn't cheering, not even smiling, and both hands are clutching her purse and she isn't saluting. I noticed her right off and I guess out of gratitude she came to pay me visits. She's in trouble: she looks old, but she isn't, she's gotten fat and her feet are giving out and her eyes are bad.

I'm here to find her. This particular ghost—proof that the past is present, if not corporeally then at least ectoplasmically. She still can't sleep. Restless, like me. I'm calling to her: across a long dead time: to touch a dark place, to scare myself a little, to make contact with what moves in the night, fifty years after, with what's driven, every night, by the panic and the pain . . .

(End of interruption.)

The Fifth Interruption was positioned between Scenes 17 and 18, where the Sixth Interruption is in the current version.

FIFTH INTERRUPTION

BERLIN 1990: VERGISS ES, VERGIEB!
(FORGIVE ME, FORGET!)

(Zillah and Roland are having a seance.)

ZILLAH

(To Roland) Hit it.

ROLAND

(Reading)
Heilig Wesen! Gestört hab' ich die goldene

Götterruhe dir oft, und der geheimeren,
Tiefern Schmerzen des Lebens
Hast du manche gelernt von mir.

[Holy Being! Often have I disturbed your golden, godlike repose, and the secret, deeper pains of life, some of which you have learned from me.]

ZILLAH

Anything? Anything?
(She thumbs through a pocket Larousse German dictionary)
Geist? Ist da eine geist in zu haus? Halo? Wer ist da?
More.

ROLAND

(Reading)
O vergiss es, vergieb! Gleich dem Gewolke dort
Vor dem friedlichen Mond, geh' ich dahin, und du
Ruhst und glänzest in deiner
Schöne wieder, du süsses Licht!

[Oh forget, forgive! The clouds before the peaceful moon, I go there, and you rest and shine in your beauty again, you sweet light! (The poem is by Hölderlin, and the translation is grotesquely literal.)]

(A pause. Agnes is in the apartment. The two women sense each other's presence.)

ZILLAH

Sssshhhh.

ROLAND

Die Mäuse?

ZILLAH

Ja, ja. Eine maus.

Sometimes at nights now I hear her moving around, sort of shuffling, patching cracks, moving things, looking for some lost object.

(Agnes moves to the cupboard, opens drawers, looks out the window.)

ZILLAH

Heavy steps, hardly the heart to move her feet. I ask her what her name was.

(Agnes stops moving, looks around the room, sensing something.)

ZILLAH

She stops moving, so I know she hears me. No answer. I ask her how she died.

(Agnes stops moving completely, frightened.)

ZILLAH

An air raid? In the camps? Because I know she died then, unhappy. Again, she doesn't move, and she hasn't answered me yet but when she does I already know what she'll say: "Not in the camps, and not in the war, but at home, in front of a cozy fire, I died of a broken heart."

(Agnes gasps.)

AGNES

Hello? Hello? Who's . . .
Oh dear God I need to sleep.

(Agnes flees from the room, Zillah rushes to where she heard Agnes gasp. Roland sneaks up behind Zillah.)

ROLAND

Boo!

ZILLAH

(Screams, then) Oy oy oy vey is mir! Meshuginah kraut!

(End of interruption.)

There was no interruption between Scenes 18 and 19.

The Sixth Interruption was positioned between Scenes 22 and 23.

SIXTH INTERRUPTION

BERLIN 1990: TREFFPUNKT (TURNING POINT)

ZILLAH

Airplane ticket.

ROLAND

Lufthansamaschine.

ZILLAH

Auf Wiedersehen.

ROLAND

Goodbye.

ZILLAH

What a year, huh? Germany reunites, Russia has a famine, and America starts World War III. And they say God has no sense of humor.

I have to go. I've met my doppelgänger. Here. *(She points to her heart)*

ROLAND

Herz.

ZILLAH

Finish the story. See it through to the end. And then go home.

ROLAND

Heim. Wohnung. New York City. Phantastisch.

ZILLAH

Neo-refugee. I go where things are falling apart, not coming together; I don't wanna be a settler, I wanna be an un-settler. Head for the bad weather, the turbulent air. Where the nightbats fly. Where you can see the danger.

(Agnes enters.)

ZILLAH

(Seeing Agnes) . . . if there's safety anywhere, it's there.

(Roland leaves. End of interruption. From this point till the end of the play, Zillah remains onstage, watching the final events.)

The Seventh Interruption was positioned between Scenes 24 and 25, where the Eighth Interruption is in the current version.

SEVENTH INTERRUPTION

BERLIN 1990: LULLABY

(Zillah and Agnes alone.)

ZILLAH

There's a terror that skips
over the mind and out the throat
faster than thinking:
Revelation: We
are in danger.
It catches us by surprise,
on beautifully sweet evenings
when we're most thoroughly
at home,
and says look
for the cracks
where the seams don't meet,
look where the walls
have moved slightly apart,
try to see, stay awake,
there isn't time for sleeping.
Hören? Kannst du mich hören?
Before the sky and the ground
slam shut. . . . Now.

(End of interruption.)

If this version of the interruptions is used, Zillah's lines at the end of the Epilogue should read:

ZILLAH

Home. Now. An end to the exile.
Before the sky and the ground slam shut.
The borders are full of holes.

AFTERWORD

The Left characterizes the Right's nostalgia as senescent; the Right characterizes the Left's demands for change as adolescent. There is some accuracy in this. The Left historically is more dependent on the energy of the young; the Right is often older (Young Republican has always seemed oxymoronic). And hence the Right is dismissed as obsolete and over-the-hill, the Left as immature.

If this is ageist I apologize for it; it's certainly too schematic. Both Left and Right have young and old adherents, and since the sixties a clean-cut generational political division, if it ever really existed, has broken down (old hippie Lefties versus young Yuppie scum or skinheads, Pete Seeger versus Axl Rose). The Right looks ahead: It has been thoroughly radical since mid-century, dismantling societies and social structures in the name of profit with a revolutionary ruthlessness that Stalin and Mao and the Khmer Rouge could envy. The Left—the true, progressive

Left—has taken increasingly to looking back longingly towards times of less-unjust injustices, less-toxic toxicity, as the Right continues to career human society forward into a future nobody wants. Right and Left, young and old are categories too simple and undialectical to be properly descriptive; and yet it is a truth, I think, that any partisan position on the political spectrum is stigmatized generally as being either pre- or post-maturity.

Maturity, according to the American politics of relativism, arrives when one believes in nothing too deeply, when one is not particularly or passionately partisan, when one hews to the gray middle, a place towards which many people are expected to drift as they approach middle age.

It is immature, certainly, to write a play which asks an audience, among other things, to consider comparisons between Ronald Reagan and Adolf Hitler. *A Bright Room Called Day* is an immature play.

Bright Room was originally published by Broadway Play Publishing in 1988, in an anthology edited by Mac Wellman entitled *Seven Different Plays* (and indeed they were). Mac asked each playwright to contribute an essay to the volume. I want to insert here the opening paragraphs of mine:

Five separate events, occurring consecutively over a short period of time, precipitated the writing of *A Bright Room Called Day*:

1. Carl Weber, the German director and translator with whom I had trained at New York University, and from whom I have learned much of what I know about theatre, was leaving New York to begin a teaching job at Stanford University in California. I felt abandoned, and I compensated for Carl's departure by acquiring a huge appetite for histories, novels and plays about German

refugees in the 1930s (I didn't unmask the source of this fixation till much later; I am slow about such things).

2. The theatre collective of which I was a founding member, and with which my best work had been done, fell apart, suffering an abrupt and anticlimactically silent demise after four years of noisy and frequently productive existence. That the group had disintegrated under pressures of no money and everyone's insufficiently analyzed craziness seemed an ominous predictor of the likely fate of any future collective enterprise. The alternative, life in the mainstream commercial theatre, looked appropriately grim.

3. My best friend and frequent collaborator, Kimberly Flynn, was seriously injured in a cab accident; and

4. My great-aunt Florence, a remarkable, loving, generous woman, died suddenly on the eve of

5. Ronald Reagan's reelection.

The winter of 1984–85 was a season of calamity. The desolate political sphere mirrored in an exact and ugly way an equally desolate personal sphere. With a grim relentlessness that now seems almost magical, every day brought news of either global failure or some intimate loss. The literature about Germany I was voraciously consuming began to savor nastily of the prophetic. Brecht's description of his era, "When there was injustice only / And no rebellion," seemed frighteningly applicable to the present.

One day in December, nearing the end of this unhappy time, I was looking at an exhibition of De Mille memorabilia (Cecil B.'s and Agnes's) at Lincoln Center. A videotape was on display, showing Agnes de Mille at work on a new dance she was choreographing, at a very advanced age, for the Joffrey Ballet. I was standing at the opposite end of the room, far from the tape, but

I thought I heard the venerable Ms. de Mille tell her interviewer that the title of the new dance was "A Bright Room Called Day." This sounded like fun and solace so I went over to watch the videotape, only to discover that the title of the piece was actually "A Bridegroom Called Death." From a bright room called day to a bridegroom called death: The metamorphosis was emblematic of the times.

My mishearing stayed with me, and eventually it came to sound like the right/wrong title of a play I had decided to write, a play about Germans, refugee and otherwise, caught on the cusp of the historic catastrophe about to engulf them. The setting may have been inspired by Carl Weber's departure, while the disintegration of our theatre company may have helped dictate the basic plot: A small circle of close friends dissolves, suddenly and silently, in the malevolent atmosphere of the day. For my friend Kimberly I wrote the part of Rosa Malek; in her clarity, intelligence, courage and commitment, Rosa resembles Kim, and Rosa escapes from Berlin. I didn't realize it at the time, but in that flight is expressed my hope that Kim will escape the worst consequences of the injuries she sustained in the accident. I named the main character Agnes, out of gratitude for Ms. de Mille's transformed title. Now I can see that Agnes is my aunt Florence (we called her Aunt Bops). It's not an exact portrait, but a profile—good, trusting, well-intended, naive. And Reagan's reelection: Then as now, I see in Reagan's career a kindred phenomenon to Hitler's accession to power.

I never indulged in fantasies of some archaic form of fascism goose-stepping down the streets of America. Reagan and the forces gathered about him seemed to me, in the flush of their demoralizing victory in 1984, the advance guard of a new and more dangerous and destructive form of barbarism, whether fascist or not. Marcuse writes, in *Counterrevolution and Revolt*:

History does not repeat itself exactly, and a higher stage of capitalist development in the United States would call for a higher stage of fascism. This country possesses economic and technical resources for a totalitarian organization immeasurably greater than Hitler Germany ever had.

Postmodern, cybernetic, microwave, microchip fascism may not look anything like its modernist forebear. Marcuse lists, among other factors inhibiting the growth of American fascism, the lack of "charismatic leaders," but the book was written in 1972. Since then, the sweaty, unappealing Nixonian conservative has been replaced by something more marketable—The Great Communicator.

In April 1985 some of the survivors of that doomed experiment in theatrical collectivity regrouped to form a new company, Heat & Light, this time on terms slightly less collective. Our first production was *A Bright Room Called Day*. Reagan's landslide reelection was six months old. The Great Communicator had by this point in his second term mined the harbor of Managua without Congressional approval and in defiance of a World Court injunction to desist, making America an outlaw nation. While we were rehearsing the play he traveled to Germany and laid tributary wreaths on the graves of S.S. soldiers in Bitburg. The unimaginable was becoming the lead story on the national news. The sixties revolution, the civil rights revolution, the feminist and lesbian and gay revolution, the Great Society, even the New Deal were being rolled back and seemed in danger of being swept away. *The Late Great Planet Earth*, a Christian fundamentalist lunatic wet dream about the role thermonuclear bombs might play in the coming armageddon and rapture, was reported to be the book with which Reagan read himself to sleep (in 1984 he'd joked on-mike just prior to a national radio broadcast that he would bomb the Soviet Union). Pat Buchanan was in the White House, George "America will not play Hamlet!" Shultz replaced Al "I'm in charge here!" Haig as Secretary of State, Cap Weinberger was developing and marketing SDI, and we hadn't even met Oliver North yet. Or seen the first baleful gleamings of Bush's "thousand points of light."

Meanwhile the AIDS epidemic was in its fifth year in America. Thousands were dead or dying, the plague was gathering force. The President, up to the time this play was written and for several years to follow, had nothing to offer the sick or the endangered, nothing in the way of funding, no public declaration of solidarity and support, not even words of ordinary rage or grief, not even mild distress. (And when his silence became too appalling and his inaction was creating civic unrest, and when it became clear that even white straight men could get AIDS, Reagan spoke and acted without conviction or sufficiency.)

At the time of its first productions, despite the evidence of such criminality and chicanery, despite the evidence of such a genocidal indifference to human life, *Bright Room* seemed even to its author to be making an outrageous comparison. And every appearance the play has made, in America and in London, has been greeted by outrage—not by audiences, who were able for the most part to integrate Zillah's rant with the issues addressed by the rest of the play—but by the critics, virtually *all* the critics. Mostly the reviews have focused on the manifest absurdity of Zillah's Reagan/Hitler metaphor; the rest of the script (the preponderance of the script) was dismissed as simply uninteresting. (The critics in Chicago, I must mention, were an exception, and so were a few critics in San Francisco.) In London, for which performances I substituted Mad Margaret Thatcher for Reagan, critics were affronted on behalf of the P.M.; in

America, some took the time to refute what they imagined to be my dire warnings that the Black Shirts were coming, while others merely sneered. Everywhere the notion of making a comparison between Reaganism and Nazism was labeled immature.

Owing to certain features of my psyche, the specifics of which I'll spare you, I'm highly susceptible to charges of immaturity; I suspect myself of it in so many ways. I admire precision while being only rarely able to manage it myself. I admire and yearn for *wisdom*, the understanding time brings to people who have spent enough years on earth with their eyes open. It has always seemed to me that wisdom implied a kind of balance—not relativism, but an ability to maintain passionate engagement in the face of the innumerable obstacles the world places before it: what Brecht called "long anger" (or maybe long love or joy). I am sometimes embarrassed by Left hyperbolism, even if I recognize the fundamental truth behind it; even though I share the anger and fear and frustration, born of the Right's cynical underestimation of every genuine social evil, which fuels our exaggerations. More often than not, what at first seems exaggerated turns out to be only a reasonable approximation of reality, even if the details aren't exact. I am of the Left because my experience of the world is that things are horribly wrong; being progressive is about being willing to admit that things are horribly wrong, is about being unable to afford to be silent; conservatives and reactionaries declare that the world's biggest problem is that poor, disenfranchised, oppressed people complain excessively.

Six years after I'd written *Bright Room*, after the secret government run by the goons of the National Security Council had made a mockery of the Constitution; after the horror of the Gulf War, and after the reportage of that war had been successfully squelched by the Pentagon; after the Rust gag rules and the sinister strangling of the NEA, the NEH and PBS; after repeated

acts of contempt for Congress by the three Reaganite adminis-
trations; after thirteen years of the counterrevolution, with the
wealth of the country having drifted exclusively into the hands
of the rich, with homeless people on every street, with the
infrastructure and the economy and education and hope col-
lapsing, even as faithful and mature a civil servant as John Frohn-
mayer (former chairman of the NEA) was standing up in public
and using the "f" word, warning that the stench of Fascism was
in the air.

I had always intended Zillah's speeches to polarize an audience, separating those who saw the value in holding a miscreant
like Reagan up to an agreed-upon standard of Evil from those
who felt such an exercise to be preposterous and jejune. Were
I writing *Bright Room* now I'd do it differently, but I wouldn't
and couldn't write *Bright Room* now. I think the play's experiment remains useful and entertaining. And while I am wary of
a tendency, given the absence of God, to substitute the judgment of History for the judgment of Heaven, I believe that
History will judge Reagan and Bush harshly; not occupying the
same circle of Hell as Hitler, but numbered among the damned.
Certainly they'll be numbered among the worst Presidents this
country has had—and we have had some stinkers.

(And speaking of stinkers: As I write this, we are burying
Nixon, the appalling paranoiac creep, the McCarthyite red-
baiter, the vindictive undignified sleazeball, the Cointelpro
crypto-fascist, the perjurer, the unindicted co-conspirator, the
carpet-bomber, the napalmer, the terminator of democracy in
Chile, the author of Cambodia's slide towards holocaust, the
friend and supporter of Brezhnev and Ceaucescu and Pinochet
and Kissinger. As Nixon's remains were consigned to the earth
at Yorba Linda, the "mature" voice was everywhere in the land,
offering balanced, gray eulogistic versions of his life and times,
unrecognizable to anyone with a memory: Nixon the super-

diplomat, Nixon the peacemaker, Nixon the intellectual giant, Nixon the lonely guy who needed to be loved. When it addresses itself to the right subjects, the mature voice begins to rasp and quaver, revealing slippage, a slide towards a dangerous forgetfulness, towards senility.)

I'm not advocating a politics of bipolar hysterical reactivity; but surely one of History's lessons, taught as eloquently and awfully through the Holocaust as any other event in human history, is that we must be wary of our attachment to the illusory comfort of our rooms, the enormous familiar weight of everyday life—we must be wary of overvaluing stability. I remember reading an interview last year in the *New York Times* with Paul Wellstone, the progressively minded Senator from Vermont, who was chastised by his fellow Senators, when, during his first week in Washington, he refused to shake the hand of Jesse Helms. Wellstone said that he now understands this refusal to be a lapse in a necessary collegiality. It almost makes one long for the days when Federal legislators used to beat each other with gutta-percha canes. Is the proffered hand of Jesse Helms not worthy of recoil? Must *every* hand be shaken? It's too easy to say that Wellstone and Helms are basically serving the same masters, and hence are only nominally differentiated members of the same clubhouse. American democracy may be a clubhouse, but its walls are coming down. Politics are not clubhouse rules of etiquette. The differences between progressive and reactionary politics are differences of life and death. When faced with a choice between the two, one must respond decisively, with passion. Better to be a Zillah than an Agnes.

When I wrote the 1988 introductory essay for *Bright Room* my concerns were twofold: whether the metaphoric principle on which Zillah's politics is based is essentially valid; and whether or not the play is politically effective art. I conclude with the final paragraphs from that essay:

It remains a question for me whether the play, which is supposed to be about morbidity and mysticism in the face of political evil, is actually to an extent a manifestation of the kind of reaction it seeks to describe. Flat, unconvincingly optimistic rhetoric is as inimical to good political theatre as is bourgeois despair (and I believe that there is such an animal, a middle-class predilection for the goose-pimply, lump-in-your-throat thrill of nihilism from which I have certainly not been exempt). When I was writing *Bright Room* all optimism felt flat and unconvincing, and despair, regardless of its class affiliations, was the order of the day. I concentrated on the history of the last phase of the collapse of the Weimar Republic, rather than on the crimes of the Third Reich, intending to rescue the play from hopelessness by showing a period of choices, when things might have turned out very differently if only. . . . The play's story ends before the worst nightmare begins, but its ending looks to the camps, the bombings, and even to the Bomb. After one of its performances in April of 1985, a man in the audience asked me whether, if I saw our situation as being a retreading of the path followed by Germany in the thirties, I saw any hope or point in resisting. The play is intended as a warning signal, not a prediction, but I often ask myself: Is it politically effective? Will it galvanize an audience to action or, less ambitiously, will it make an audience think, argue, examine the present through the example of the past? Or will it merely confirm and voice for them what they may already suspect: That something unstoppable and horrendous is right around the corner?

There's a great scene in Bergman's *The Seventh Seal* between Jons, the knight's sidekick and serving-man, and a mural painter in a country church:

Jons: What is that supposed to represent?

Painter: The Dance of Death.

Jons: And that one is death?

Painter: Yes, he dances off with all of them.

Jons: Why do you paint such nonsense?

Painter: I thought it would serve to remind the people that they must die.

Jons: Well, it's not going to make them feel any happier.

Painter: Why should one always make people happy? It might not be a bad idea to scare them a little once in a while.

Jons: Then they'll close their eyes and refuse to look at your painting.

Painter: Oh, they'll look. A skull is almost more interesting than a naked woman *[apologies for the sexism—TK]*.

Jons: If you scare them . . .

Painter: They'll think.

Jons: And if they think . . .

Painter: They'll become still more scared.

Jons: And then they'll run right into the arms of the priests.

Painter: That's not my business.

Jons: You're only painting your Dance of Death.

Painter: I'm only painting things as they are. Everyone else can do as he likes.

Jons: Just think how some people will curse you.

Painter: Maybe. But then I'll paint something amusing for them to look at. I have to make a living—at least until the plague takes me.

This painter is not a responsible political artist. He is, however, political, as Jons points out, as we all are, whether or not we choose to be, till the plague takes us.

Not everyone who refuses the designation "political artist" wants to send his or her audience into the arms of the priests, and many such people have created powerfully progressive political work. Conversely, it is not unusual for someone who embraces this designation to accomplish nothing finer than terrifying others, which is more likely to promote prayer than activism. There is always the balancing trick, difficult to manage, of portraying powerlessness and empowerment at the same time, of evoking Hell without its traditional concomitant, eternal damnation.

[I am less sure, in 1994, that prayer is the antithesis of activism; I recommend both.]

Because *Bright Room* grew out of a period of grief and of mourning losses, I haven't found a way to make it more "positive" without being false to what's there, much of which I like. But grief and mourning don't lie beyond the reach of history. All through that benighted year during which the play was written I became less and less politically active. I was losing my connection with activism because of an indolence born out of . . . well, indolence, but also perhaps out of fear, out of a sense of being overwhelmed, as a character in the play says. I'm certain that my stagnation in the realm of active involvement has had a tidal effect on the way the world presents itself to me, changing the face of the enemy from something fearsome into something irresistible. It's not that you don't have a right to write about issues of active resistance when you aren't actively resisting; it's more important that a removal from the struggle distorts any analysis of the struggle—distance, in this instance, does not equal clarity. A resurgence of activism has altered the shape and tenor of the play. So did Oskar Eustis's suggestion that I "complexify" the despair.

Through further research I learned that 80,000 Communists died in German concentration camps. The loss of life, and the lost battle that loss implies, are well worth despairing over, but the fact of such extraordinary resistance carries its own weighty imperative. The history of the Weimar Republic is more than a story of ineffectual decency and ascendant evil, more than the story of its impressive refugees. It is also the story of a heroic resistance that sends, from the mass graves, a mandate to the present, which speaks against the dangerous illusion of the inevitable unsuccess of opposition to oppression.

When we conjure up the past we run the risk of reawakening old nightmares, of being overwhelmed with horror. Conjuring the future is even more treacherous, because to attempt to envision the future we must resort to what is known, to the past, and if the past *as* past is nearly unbearable, how much more unbearable to look ahead and see only old nightmares staring back at us. Then again, considering the dire present, imagining that we have any future at all has got to be accounted a cause for celebration.

Those who govern us, in whose hands power is most concentrated, have as their objective, if we can judge by their actions, to bring time to an end, to abolish past and future. That this is so, that these people are who they are, that we have permitted them to wield such power and may permit worse yet, is so fundamentally threatening that we reject immediate knowledge of it. In the grip of that knowledge, every human action, including the making of theatre, would have to be directed toward the abolition of such power and of the systems that maintain it. The brightest hope for the future would be any event, theatrical and otherwise, that presses this knowledge closer to home.